BRITAIN'S LOST WATERWAYS

Thomas Beard was the last barge owner
to trade on the upper reaches of the
River Severn, and this photograph of
his boat *William* of Broseley, is thought
to have been taken in 1895. The
location is opposite the Jackfield Kilns
of the Maws tile works. The trow is
moored on the Coalport bank. Clearly
seen is the yard for the square rig. The
square stern and extreme width of these
upper river trows is shown, also the
wash cloths, which would have been
spread along the gunwale to give
increased height, also to stop water
coming inboard.

HISTORIC WATERWAYS SCENES

BRITAIN'S LOST WATERWAYS

Michael E Ware

MOORLAND PUBLISHING

British Library Cataloguing in Publication Data
Ware, Michael E.
  Britain's lost waterways. — 2nd ed.
  1. Great Britain. Canals, history
  I. Title
  386'.46'0941

ISBN 0 86190 327 7

First published 1979 as two volumes
New single-volume edition 1989

Published by
Moorland Publishing Co Ltd
Moor Farm Road West
Ashbourne, Derbyshire DE6 1HD

Printed in Great Britain

CONTENTS

ACKNOWLEDGEMENTS

So many people have helped with this book that it would not be possible to list them all. First and foremost thanks must go to Edward Paget-Tomlinson for so kindly reading everything that was written, correcting it in many places and as usual adding many interesting and absorbing facts. Many people with local knowledge checked the pages on their particular waterways. In particular I would like to thank Major C.B. Grundy, Brian Waters, Peter Norton, Alan Faulkner, David Robinson, John Goodchild, Humphrey Household, Kenneth Clow, David Winter, Ian L. Wright, Alan Oxtaby, David McDougal, and the staff of the Ironbridge Gorge Museum Trust. Michael Sedgwick corrected the grammatical mistakes while Paulette Hinchin not only wrote over 550 research letters but typed the manuscript at least twice. I am very grateful to my wife Janet, for all the helpful comments she has made, and the encouragement she has given me. Much inspiration and help has been gained from Ronald Russell's excellent book *Lost Canals of England and Wales*.

As to the picture research, this has been done over a two-year period during which time I must have looked at well over 60,000 photographs. There are 30,000 pictures in the Francis Frith Collection alone, and I went right through them thanks to the enthusiasm of John Buck. The greatest find must have been those photographs within the archives of the former Great Western Railway, administered by Jim Russell. Jim allowed me unrestricted access to his registers and indexes and from these have come many photographs which have not previously been reproduced in books about canals. As for those million photographs in the National Monument Record, I can only claim to have scraped the surface. Richard Hutchings, former Curator of the Waterways Museum at Stoke Bruerne, gave much encouragement and lent many photographs from that museum's collection. I have again used a number of pictures from the extensive collection of Hugh McKnight.

The author and publisher are grateful to the following for the use of illustrations:

Part 1
J. Anderson: 80; Mrs J. Beech: 69, 70; Birmingham Museum of Science and Industry: 31; Black Country Museum: 44; Bradford Central Library: 127, 128; British Rail, Midland Region: 114; British Rail, Western Region: 26, 60, 61, 62, 63; J.E. Brownlow: 85; Derby Museum: 15; Derby Public Library: 12, 13; Derbyshire Record Office: 16, 97; John Dickinson & Co Ltd: 141; Dudley Canal Trust: 42; Dudley Public Library: 46, (T.W. King Collection): 40, 45, 47; Francis Frith Collection: 1, 33, 111; W.K.V. Gale: 41; Grantham Library: 81; A.R. Griffin: 2; Alan Griffiths: 140; Charles Hadfield: 88; Hampshire County Museums Service: 48, 49, 50; Harmsworth Family Collection: 52, 58; H. Harris: 79; Hereford Library: 64, 65; A. Hulme: 136; Ironbridge Gorge Museum Trust: 76, 78; E. Jones (via Lady Markham): 116, 117, 118; Kendal Library: 108, 112; G. Knapp, 82; Leicester Museums: 132; Peter Lewis, 67, 68; Mack of Manchester Ltd: 137; C. Makepeace: 105; Eric de Maré: 29; Hugh McKnight Collection: 34, 35, 36, 37, 71, 83, 87, 102, 103, 107, 109, 110, 113, 139; National Coal Board: 3; National Monument Record: 73, 125; Peter Norton: 95; H. Northern: *Frontis*, , 53, 56; *Old Motor:* 77; H.W. Plant:135; C.L.M. Porter: 91, 92, 93, 94; Rochdale Canal Company: 21, 22; Rochdale Metropolitan Borough Library: 17, 23, 24, 25; Frank Rodgers: 11, 14, 84, 99, 100; L.T.C. Rolt archives: 27, 28, 38; Stafford Museum: 126; Surrey and Hampshire Canal Society Archives: 51; Mrs Temple Thurston: 30; City of Wakefield Metropolitan District Archives, Goodchild loan MSS: 4, 6, 7, 9; Waterways Museum, Stoke Bruerne: 32, 66, 74, 75, 98, 101, 103, 106, 115, 119, 121, 123, 124, 129, 130, 131; Reginald Wood: 18, 19, 20.

Part 2
Abingdon Museum: 51; Aero Films Ltd: 5, 8; Harry Arnold: 119; D.H.R. Bird: 55; Brede Women's Institute: 127; British Railways, Western Region: 6, 13, 14, 16-19, 21, 40, 58, 60-1, 74-9, 81-6, 101-2, 129; British Waterways Museum, Stoke Bruerne: 91; Chesterfield Canal Society: 123; Chesterfield Central Library: 121-2; Capt H.J. Chubb (per E. Paget-Tomlinson): 45-6; Corinium Museum, Cirencester (per D. Viner): 35; Cynon Valley Borough Library: 64-5, 68, 71-2; East Sussex Libraries (Hastings): 128; Francis Frith Collection: 133; Gloucestershire Records Office: 27, 36, 41, 43, 48-9; John Gould: 87; J.S. Gray: 110; W.E.R. Hallgarth: 124; Hertfordshire County Records Office: 90; Humphrey Household: 31-2, 34, 50; Ironbridge Gorge Museum Trust: *Frontis*, 134-5, 137; Liverpool City Museum: 118; Hugh McKnight Collection: 10, 25, 44; Manchester Ship Canal: 116, 117; Mansell Collection: 47; Eric de Maré: 4; David Miller: 54; Morwellham Quay Open Air Museum: 97-8; Museum of English Rural Life, Reading: 92-4; National Monuments Record: 26, 33, 100, 131-2; National Museum of Wales: 67; Peter Norton: 112, 115; Michael Norris Hill: 103, 105; P.T. Oke (per E. Paget-Tomlinson): 95; Oxfordshire County Libraries: 53; E. Paget-Tomlinson: 113, 114; Pilkington Glass Museum (Pilkington Brothers Ltd): 111; Pontypridd Public Library: 59, 63; L.T.C. Rolt archives: 20; Shrewsbury Library: 136; *South Wales Echo:* 69-70; *Stroud News & Journal* (per D. Viner): 43; Swindon Library: 56-7; Swindon Museum: 52; Mrs Temple Thurston: 23-4, 38-9; Watts, Blake, Bearne & Co Ltd: 96; Philip Weaver: 28; Reece Winstone, FRPS: 22, 66. Illustrations not otherwise acknowledged are from the author's collection.

PREFACE

An author of books of this sort is lucky; he can make his own rules. That is all very well; but he must also explain the rules to the readers, if he and his publisher are not to be inundated with letters from canal enthusiasts saying that their favourite piece of waterway has been omitted. These books were to have been entitled 'Forgotten Waterways', but it was soon realised that this would upset all those hard workers who are currently striving to re-open long disused canals and other navigations. Rude reviews would be written (they still may be, of course!) in club or association journals.

The rough criterion for a waterway's inclusion in the book is that it has been closed at one time or another. In some cases the closure may not have been official. In a number of cases, I am pleased to say, the canals have subsequently been re-opened to traffic. Wherever possible the canals have been depicted in the days when they were carrying commercial craft, the traffic for which they were built. In a few cases pictures are included of derelict canals, but in the main these were photographed so long ago as to be of interest to the enthusiast as well as the industrial archaeologist. Only a very few modern pictures of such waterways appear.

In undertaking my research I tried to find sources of illustrations for practically every canal which has closed. Having gathered them all together I found it quite impossible to illustrate each one and anyway this process would have been repetitive in the extreme. I have therefore chosen those pictures which in my opinion best reflect the overall scene, even if this meant the inclusion of a disproportionate number from any one individual canal. I hope I have included your favourite but if I have not, then blame it on these rules.

I think I must have written to most of the societies and associations which are connected with closed waterways. I have received many helpful and knowledgeable replies. I have been surprised, though, at the number of societies who do not appear to have a member whose job it is to research and collect historic items of print or illustration. My request to one society nearly produced solicitor's letters between two members who did hold such photographs but for internal political reasons found themselves unable to make them available! If these books do nothing else, I hope they will make such societies more aware of this particular branch of waterway history. The collection of such material is best done in collaboration with the local history society, library, museum, or county records office; thus the maximum benefit will result to all.

Because of the amount of material collected this work will appear in two parts. Those canals and navigations which are basically internal are included in this volume. The second part will contain those navigations which go down to the sea, and will include the canals of South Wales and the waterways which link the River Thames with the Severn and its estuary.

In this book I have drawn on two major works of reference, quoting extensively from each. Of these Priestley's *Navigable Rivers and Canals,* first published in 1831, gives an account of each canal and railway for the construction of which an Act of Parliament was passed in or before 1830. Secondly, *Bradshaw's Canals and Navigable Rivers of England and Wales* by Henry Rodolph de Salis; this was first published in 1904, and lists all canals which were navigable in that year, giving details of the route, locks, wharves, tunnels, junctions and most other topographical features, as well as the principal dimensions of the boats that could trade on them. To do this de Salis, who was a director of the canal carrying company Fellows Morton and Clayton, travelled over 14,000 miles by water, mainly in his steam launch *Dragon Fly.* These trips took him 11 years. Little credit has been given to de Salis as a photographer, and while he may not have been technically very efficient, many of the pictures he took on this trip have survived. They are in the collection of Hugh McKnight and a number are used in this book. Very few working boatmen kept a diary, hence for descriptions of trips on canals in the last century or early in this we must rely on the accounts of a few upper class travellers who took to the canals for a holiday. I have quoted from E. Temple Thurston's book *The Flower of Gloster,* an account of such a trip in 1908. His widow is happily still alive and has allowed me access to the photographic record of his trip. (All three of these books have been made available in recent years as reprints by David and Charles of Newton Abbot).

INTRODUCTION

Introduction to Part 1

When the Duke of Bridgewater's Canal was opened in 1761 the price of coal in Manchester is reputed to have fallen from 7d to 4d a hundredweight. We can marvel at the actual prices quoted but this drop of nearly 50 per cent in the charges demonstrates better than anything else the effect the canal had on the urban population of Manchester. It is a pity the coming of North Sea oil has not had a similar effect on our life today.

Before the advent of the canal system overland transport in Britain had been very difficult. The Romans had given us a first-rate road system, but once they had left there was no central government to take responsibility for it. A need for trade has always existed although for many years it was confined to essentials such as salt, wool or corn. The roads were so poor that coal would normally only be carried for a few miles around the colliery or bellpit. Packhorse trains could not carry any great quantity of materials although they could traverse poor roads. Any form of cart required a reasonable surface on which to travel.

River navigation was important but because of floods and rapids most rivers needed artificial attention to allow boats to travel any real distance inland. If we take the Thames as an example, by the early Middle Ages it was navigable only as far as Richmond, and even by 1660 Oxford marked the upper limit. The Thames above Oxford was to be a tricky navigation until the 1900s. One of the biggest problems with rivers was the presence of mills, each of which required a head of water to operate. Understandably, millers were reluctant to let the water impounded behind their dam or weir flow freely just to allow a barge to pass up or down stream.

The Duke of Bridgewater's canal from his coalmines at Worsley was not the country's first artificial waterway but it was the start of the great Midland system — Trent and Mersey, Staffordshire and Worcestershire, etc. There is no denying the Bridgewater's effect on industry and local people around Manchester. Coal could travel over the 11-mile canal day and night with virtually no hindrance from weather, mill owners or other disruptions. Even while this canal was being built industrialists were recognising its potential, and its engineers, John Gilbert and James Brindley, were in great demand for new projects. Within the next forty years or so 'canal mania' set in. Nearly every city, town or village wanted a waterway. It is interesting to note that Parliament looked enthusiastically on the majority of the projects, as the Canal Acts came before them. They fully realised that if private enterprise did not do it, they might be asked to subsidise some of them from Government funds. Many were built, but equally many were never started; other projects were started but never completed. The Southampton to Salisbury canal and the Leominster canal would be good examples of the latter. The canals held sway until the early 1850s, by which time the railways had become firmly established. Many of the canal companies had only themselves to blame for the loss of much of their trade to the railways. For fifty or so years they had enjoyed a monopoly. Some had charged high tolls, or had paid excellent dividends to the shareholders. Many had ploughed insufficient money back into maintenance or had failed to plan for expansion; in other words, complacency set in. Telford is reputed to have made the following comment in the 1820s on the state of the Birmingham canals, saying that they had become

. . . little better than a crooked ditch, with scarcely the appearance of a towing-path, the horses frequently sliding and staggering in the water, the hauling-lines sweeping the gravel into the canal, and the entanglement at the meeting of boats being incessant; whilst at the locks at each end of the short summit at Smethwick crowds of boatmen were always quarrelling, or offering premiums for a preference of passage; and the mine-owners, injured by the delay, were loud in their just complaints . . .

In the 1820s or 1830s, under Telford's direction, the Birmingham main line was greatly improved, deepened and widened; for once money was being ploughed back. The great works which took place on the Grand Union between London and Birmingham in the 1930s came a hundred years too late. Through no fault of their own, the different gauges of numerous neighbouring waterways were a cause of extra expense to traders, and had Brindley and his associates shown greater foresight, the locks on his first cross country waterway, the Trent and Mersey, would not have been fixed at 7 feet by 72 feet, so laying down the dimensions of the traditional narrow boat, which in later years had great difficulty in surviving as an economic proposition.

The view has been expressed that the Duke of Bridgewater exercised some influence over the size of locks on the Trent and Mersey and some other canals. The Duke wanted to secure the cargoes by transhipment from the smaller narrow boats into his bigger Mersey flats at Preston Brook, for onward transmission to Liverpool. It must be remembered that there was also a substantial mileage of canal and river navigation designed for larger craft, such as keels, flats, trows, etc.

Another problem was that the canal companies were not allowed to run fleets of cargo boats on their own canals. They had to rely on tolls from private traders. In 1847 this law was changed, but not all the companies took advantage of it. Those that did found in the main that they could improve their incomes by becoming carriers.

At first, narrow boats had an all-male crew who lived on the bank overnight. Later the boatmen had to take his family from the bank and put them on the boat. Here all of them were set to work, thus dispensing with the services of a mate. The family did, however, have to work unnaturally long hours — sometimes seven days a week as well — to make ends meet. From this progression we can see that the private trader was gradually forced off the water.

At first the railways were only interested in passenger traffic and the carriage of light goods, neither of which was a real threat to the waterways, who ran relatively few packet or passenger boats. Soon, however, the rail directors realised that heavy goods and mineral traffic would bring in a good revenue; then came the real clash between the two transport systems. I think it is true to say that for quite a number of years waterways kept those old customers who were on the canalside, but new factories, collieries, etc, tended to be rail-connected if this was at all possible. It was the country canals which suffered first.

They had never carried high tonnages; therefore tolls were low and so was income in relation to expenditure. The coming of the country railway hit them hard; one should remember that it has only been in the recent past that the daily pick-up goods train has departed our railways, and a daily rail connection for agricultural products is far better than slow delivery by canal.

Canals could compete as long as cargoes could be loaded directly into the boats and off-loaded direct into the factory at the other end; as long, also, as speed was of secondary importance. If a factory's requirement was 25 tons of coal a day, it did not really matter how long it took that coal to reach the factory provided the supply was regular and prices competitive. Unlike the railways, canals were often affected by weather conditions in the winter, and ice-breaking was a major part of a maintenance gang's work at such times. The waterway could be held up for weeks while the railways were relatively unaffected. Structural repairs did not usually disrupt a railway for more than a day or two, but lock or bridge repairs could close a canal for weeks on end. It must also be realised that although there were 4,000 miles of canal in 1860, there were a good 7,500 miles of railway at that time.

Although the Turnpike Acts of the 1800s led to substantial improvements, roads were not used for regular long distance heavy haulage until the 1920s, by which time the motor lorry was firmly established. The lorry was the death-blow to the canal system as far as commercial traffic was concerned in the Midlands and the South. A certain amount of coal, oil, and other products are, however, still a regular traffic on river navigations in the north-east.

These, then, were some of the pressures on the canals, and the reasons why so many closed. These two books try to capture the feel of the commercial waterway system by looking at canals which have closed or have been abandoned, and which in many cases have been all but obliterated by subsequent development.

1

1   Most of the Bridgewater Canal as originally built is still very much with us and in use, but one small section, now derelict, was very important. As we have seen, the purpose of the waterway was to bring coal from Worsley into Manchester. At first the coal was mined in the conventional way from above. Drainage is always a problem in mines and here a drainage sough (tunnel) was built from the base of the workings out of the nearby hillside at Worsley into the Worsley Brook. With the coming of the canal to Worsley this sough was made navigable so that boats could be taken right into the mines. To work within the restricted confines of these mines a new type of boat was built, known by the slang term 'starvationer'. Their proper title is 'M boats'. The nickname 'starvationer' probably came about because of the very exposed knees within the boat which when unloaded does have the appearance of a skeleton. There were three sizes of boat, the largest being 55 feet long and 4 feet 6 inches wide. It could carry 12 tons on a draught of 2 feet 6 inches. These were the forerunners of the English narrow boat. Coal was mined and placed into containers, and these containers were loaded into the boats. Is nothing new? This scene was taken around the turn of the century at Worsley Delph and shows a number of derelict M boats of different sizes. Mining had ceased in 1887.

2   The historian Samuel Smiles writes of these mines

...the barges are deeply laden with their black freight, which they have brought from the mines through the two low semi-circular arches opening at the base of the rock, such being the entrances to the underground canals which now extend to nearly 40 miles in all directions. . . . Where the tunnel passed through earth or coal the arching was of brickwork but where it passed through rock it was simply hewn out.

Trains of between six and twenty boats at a time would be taken into the mine. There were 46 miles of underground canal in all, on four levels including an inclined plane 151 feet long with a slope of one in four. What a frightening place it must have been to work in.

3 The derelict mines these days are looked after by the National Coal Board. This picture, taken in recent years, shows such an NCB inspection party emerging, having undertaken the journey in one of the old M boats. At one time a few visits were arranged in order that industrial archaeologists could inspect these workings, but the mines are said to be so dangerous now that this practice has ceased. At the end of the original length of the Bridgewater Canal in Manchester another tunnel was built. Wharves and warehouses were situated at the basin at Castlefield which was well below the main streets of the city. To save having to tranship the coal to carts and haul it laboriously up the hillside, a ¾ mile tunnel was dug into the side of the hill, and at a point near Deansgate a vertical shaft was sunk to connect with the tunnel below. The boats from Worsley were taken into the underground tunnels and 8 cwt containers unloaded by means of a crane pulling them up the shaft. Power for the crane was supplied by a waterwheel. The rate of unloading is said to have been 5 tons of cargo every half hour, which was handled by two men and a boy.

4 The Barnsley Canal left the Aire and Calder main line via Heath Lock, a mile downstream from Wakefield. With the Dearne and Dove Canal it provided a route through the prosperous South Yorkshire coalfields from the Aire and Calder to the Don Navigation. It was completed through to Barnsley in 1799; an extension right into the coal-producing area beyond to Barnby basin was opened three years later. Priestley, writing in his *Navigable Rivers and Canals* published in 1831, says,

this canal was projected principally with the view of opening the very valuable and extensive coal fields in the neighbourhood of Barnsley and Silkstone, and its execution has had the effect of introducing the coal, worked in the latter place, into the London Market, where it holds a distinguished place amongst the Yorkshire coals.

Here we see an empty Yorkshire keel rising out of Heath Lock at the entrance to the canal around the turn of this century. The lock-cum-toll keeper lived in the house; the building on the left houses the canalside stables; we see a horse coming out of one of them. The boat horse is being led by a 'horse marine' as the horsemen were always known in Yorkshire. Keels often had a coggie boat or rowing boat with them for use on tidal waters. As these were not used when trading on canals, some visiting keels have left theirs tied to the bank on the right of the picture.

CONNECTING CANALS

Most canals were planned individually. Completely separate companies were set up and there was great rivalry between them. It was not until they were in existence that some of the rivalry eased, and the advantages could be seen in making sure that trade could flow from one waterway to another and from one part of the country to another. In some cases the companies were pig-headed and situations such as that at Worcester Bar came into being. Here the Worcester and Birmingham Canal was not allowed to join the Birmingham Canal Navigations; a stretch of wharf a few yards wide was left between them, and all on-going cargoes had to be transhipped. Canal companies were always jealous of their water and when a new canal wharf joined an established one it was usually made to come in at a higher level via the entrance lock. In this way the established canal always obtained a lock full of water as each boat passed through the lock. The stop locks at Hawkesbury Junction (Oxford Canal with the Coventry Canal) and Autherley Junction (Shropshire Union Canal with the Staffordshire and Worcestershire Canal) are possibly the best examples. At Hawkesbury both canals had their own stop lock and both locks had a drop of only a few inches.

Even though they were not all connecting canals the waterways of Birmingham have been included in this section. These are really so interesting and intricate that they require a full length pictorial book of their own. It has often been quoted that there were many more miles of canal in Birmingham and the Black Country than there were in Venice. Be that as it may, the Midlands Canals were very important indeed and in general terms carried more traffic than almost any other waterway in this country.

4

Heath Locks. Wakefield.

5 Here is a view down the Aire and Calder main line, with Heath Lock toll house and the Barnsley Canal on the right. A non-tidal Yorkshire keel, most probably loaded with coal, has just left the lock. At this point the tow path of the Aire and Calder navigation was on the far bank (out of the picture on the left-hand side). The boat tied up in the foreground (extreme left) is the ferry used by boatmen to bring their horses across should they be going from the Aire and Calder onto the Barnsley Canal. The date is around 1905. The Silkstone Collieries provided much of the traffic on the canal in earlier days; this coal had to be taken by cart on the local roads to the canal head. Due to the appalling state of these roads there were often hold-ups and it was not unusual to find up to ten boats waiting at the basin for their cargoes to arrive. Later this fault was overcome by the building of a horse-drawn plateway to the canal. Some say the delay was also caused by poor output at the coal face — whatever the reason, boat owners could not afford serious delays such as this.

6 This photograph, taken around 1900, is of the Heath flight of locks with two Yorkshire keels passing. The nearer of the two vessels is one of the Aire and Calder's own carrying fleet, which were numbered but not named, and is returning empty or at least lightly loaded. Keel captains would always try to obtain the back carriage of a cargo if they possibly could. In the earlier years of the canal, limestone formed an important back loading against the down flow of coal. Possibly the white substance in the hold of the loaded boat seen here is limestone. Lime kilns were established on the sides of the canals, and some coalmasters took the opportunity to burn off their slack in these kilns. Tidal keels always towed from the neddy (towing mast) stepped in the lutchet; non-tidal versions swapped their masts from side to side depending on the towing path. It can be seen that Number 42 has laid the neddy flat and is towing from the lutchet, while the keel coming up has the neddy erect, presumably to counteract her lowness in the water. The canal had been taken over by the Aire and Calder Navigation in 1854 and later they worked traffic of up to 272,000 tons in one year.

7 Water was a problem on the Barnsley Canal. Originally an 80 acre reservoir was built at Cold Hindley, which in later years was augmented by the building of another one nearby at Wintersett. Unusually, this Cornish pumping engine at Ryhill pumping station was used to take water out of the canal whenever there was a surplus and pump it back into the reservoir for future use. The beam engine came from Harveys of Hayle and was most probably bought second-hand from a disused Cornish copper mine. It was by no means worn out, as it continued in use until the closure of the canal in 1946. Mining subsidence was a problem in the area; in 1911 the Barnsley aqueduct was affected and had to be closed for repairs for eight months. Again in 1945 there was trouble near the aqueduct. Mottram Wood colliery was flooded, and compensation had to be paid. In November 1946 the canal burst its banks at Littleworth and that really was the end, although abandonment did not come until 1953. This photograph is thought to have been taken around 1910.

11 Reservoir Engine House
Ryhill

8 This fine engraving of a colliery scene is of Edmund Main colliery to the south of Barnsley on the Worsborough branch of the Dearne and Dove Canal, opened in 1804. The sketch is dated 1859. If this drawing was taken from life, why, one wonders, did the artist depict the trading boats as having sails? Could it have been that he saw keels with masts which he thought were for sails? The boats are clearly meant to be keels, but they would only sail on canals if the wind conditions really suited them, and then only with a small square sail on a short mast. In canal work it was normal for keels to leave masts and lee boards on the bank, say at Doncaster. While coal was one of the chief traffics on the Dearne and Dove, it was also its downfall. This branch had to be closed in 1906 because of mining subsidence and parts of the canal were only 4 feet 6 inches deep when they should have been 6 feet deep, due to this same problem. The Elsecar branch was closed for the same reason in 1928.

9 The branch of the Dearne and Dove to the Elsecar basin was only just over two miles long, but had a rise of six locks. It was built principally to serve collieries. Unfortunately the date of this photograph is not known but it is a most interesting scene in the basin at Elsecar. The keel on the left has arrived loaded with pit props, while the one behind appears to be empty. These keels were fitted with close-fitting hatch boards (covers) to keep the cargoes dry from both rain and tidal water, but they often covered non-perishable cargoes as well. The covers have a very distinct curve on them which allows unladen boats the maximum amount of room under low bridges such as those on the section of the Sheffield Canal, an extension of the Don Navigation. The keel in the foreground has had its rudder lengthened to help with manoeuverability on the canals. It is also fitted with a special canal tiller bent up and over the rail. Such a tiller helps when rounding sharp bends as an ordinary one would foul the stanchions. The hefty rope in the coggie or cock boat in the foreground shows that the keels were used for trading on tidal waterways. The clinker planking of the two keels in the foreground tells us that they were built no later than the mid-19th century.

10 For once it is possible to illustrate a way in which canal water can be used to help a coalmine; usually the mines are blamed for subsidence which causes havoc with the banks and beds of waterways. There was a serious explosion at Edmund Main colliery in December 1862 when fifty-nine men and boys were killed. The owners were unable to extinguish the ensuing fire, and eventually a channel was dug from the nearby canal and the water used to flood the pit.

8

11 The line of the Derby Canal is shaped like an inverted 'V' with Derby at the apex. One arm of the canal connects with the Erewash Canal at Sandiacre, and the other end with the Trent and Mersey at Swarkestone junction — about the only point, incidentally, where the canal can be clearly seen these days. Opened in 1796, it enjoyed some through trade, but most of it went to Derby. Otherwise it was traffic from the Little Eaton branch canal — mainly coal. An interesting aspect of the canal was its crossing of the River Derwent in Derby itself. The canal crossed the river on the level just upstream of an unusual semi-circular weir. In order that the tow path could also cross, a narrow timber bridge was built. In times of flood it shielded the narrow boats from being swept over the weir but it was often being damaged itself due to the build-up of water-borne flood debris. Pedestrians were allowed to use the bridge as long as they did not 'wheel perambulators or barrows that may impede the passage of horses'. It became unsafe in 1950 and was finally demolished in 1959.

12 The coming of the canal led to the opening up of a number of waterside arms and wharves off the River Derwent itself. Just above the canal crossing there was another weir across the river, but this was by-passed by a short lock cut for water-borne traffic wanting to reach the wharves of the leadshot producing company of Cox Brothers, part of Morledge Leadworks situated on the Markeaton brook leading down to the river. Here the brook has been made navigable for Trent-type barges; one of these and a narrow boat are seen loading. The shot tower, incidentally, was built in 1809 and was demolished in 1931. Tenant Bridge is in the foreground.

13 The first lock up from the river crossing on the south side was Pegg's Flood Lock, an unusually shaped lock as the gates were at either end of a wharf area. Under normal circumstances the gates of this lock were kept open. If the river was in flood then the bottom gate would be shut to hold the river water back — the gates were mitred the opposite way to normal for this purpose. This photograph, taken in August 1874, shows Days Lock, the next one up the canal, a few hundred yards above Peggs Flood Lock. Though the fall through this lock is not very great, it too can be operated as a flood lock. In this picture it is in use in the normal way. Should flood water come up the canal from Peggs (out of the picture down the canal to the left), the extra pair of gates shown in the foreground could be closed to protect the canal above. The house on the right is the toll-and-lock keeper's cottage. One upstairs window is set noticeably higher up under the roof. This would have been the window from which the toll keeper watched for approaching traffic.

11

14 For many years the Derby Canal Company tried to sell itself to a railway company; there were, however, no takers. But before it suffered at the hands of railway competition, it had handled as much as 200,000 tons of cargo in a year, a good performance by most standards. The company tried to close the canal in the 1920s, but never actually got round to doing it. After World War II the canal was allowed to abandon itself even though officially it did not close until 1964. The canal company remained in being until June 1974, and this is a photograph of their Bridgewater Wharf in Derby. The warehouse on the right with the crane was built in 1820, and along with all the other buildings in the wharf area was demolished in July 1975. This picture was taken about 1960; the derelict craft was an ice-breaker. The photograph was taken from Cattle Market Bridge, under which once stood what was probably the first cast-iron aqueduct. It was designed by Benjamin Outram to carry the canal over an earlier cut by George Sorocold.

15

15 The Canal Tavern was situated in Cockpit Hill, approximately 200 yards from the canal wharf in Derby itself. Nearby were two other pubs, The Castle and Falcon, and The Boat. All three were demolished in the late 1960s during clearance to make way for the new Eagle Shopping Centre. This picture is thought to date from the early 1930s. The bus is a 1927 Gilford, and behind it is a splendidly ornate urinal. The public house was an important part of the boatman's life, particularly in horsedrawn days. Most canalside pubs had stables. This one, for example, offers 'good stabling' where the horse could be left overnight. The pub was the only form of recreation that boatmen would normally get; most would be working long hours and possibly six or even seven days a week as well. It would be wrong, however, to assume that the boatman's life was one long pub crawl. There would be many occasions when he could not afford even a beer in the tavern. As the canals lost their commercial traffic and closed down, so did many of the pubs, as they had no alternative market to draw on. A few situated near roads and bridges could turn

their backs on the canal and try and tempt car and coach traffic. Some of these have recently turned round again, and now obtain their trade from passing pleasure boats!

16 The part which the tramway played in the first hundred odd years of the canal system has received insufficient attention from writers. At one time there were over 1,500 miles of horsedrawn waggon or tramway in England and Wales, a large proportion of which led from quarries, mines or works down to navigable water of some sort, usually a canal or river. In many cases canals were originally designed to connect with such a tramway, usually because the terrain was difficult and it was cheaper to build a tramway than extend the canal. The Little Eaton Gangway from the Derby Canal was typical. In the original Canal Act it said '. . . and for making Railways from such canal to several collieries. . . .' Further on the Act says 'And also to make and maintain a Rail or Wagon Way or Stone Road for the conveyance of coal, iron, ironstone, lead ore, limestone and other articles . . .

from the termination of the canal at Little Eaton aforesaid. . . .' The gangway's principal cargo was coal from Denby and Kilburn collieries. The coal was loaded into containers, each box containing 33-8 cwt. At Little Eaton Wharf the gangs of loaded trams were positioned in such a way that the wharf crane could unload them into the waiting narrow boats. The Little Eaton Company was one of the last to close, and this picture of pointwork by the Wharf was taken in 1908, a year before closure.

17 The state of the roads over the Pennines from Manchester to Yorkshire in the mid 1700s can be imagined, so it is not surprising that one of the first canal schemes mooted in the north would follow that route. It took a long time, however, before the Rochdale Canal became a *fait accompli*, and it was not until 1804 that it was opened from Manchester through to join the Calder and Hebble at Sowerby Bridge. The canal was built to wide dimensions of 14 feet 2 inches and the locks were 72 feet in length, so most types of northern inland trading craft could traverse it. Here we see a pair of narrow boats breasted up at Clegg Hall, Littleborough. These narrow boats were deep (six planks instead of the usual five) and could be said to be clumsy. The gang plank at the forend rests on a stand and not a triangular cratch as is more common on the Midland narrow boat. The date of the picture is not known, neither is it known why the boats are facing in opposite directions!

18 One of the most successful traders on the Rochdale Canal was William Jackson, who in 1845 had over 30 barges or flats trading. It is interesting to see that he also had 120 horses, which averages out at 4 per boat, the reason for this high number being that fly boats (express boats) required frequent changes of horses, and many spare horses were always kept. In 1891 he sold out to the Rochdale Canal Company. In 1894 two of these boats were bought by Albert Wood of Sowerby Bridge. This photograph, taken at Castleton near Rochdale in 1907, shows Albert Wood's Mersey flat *Bedford*, typical of the craft which would have traded in the area. Such boats were a very tight fit into the locks, hence the elaborate sets of fenders — both sill and stem types. This would have been a family boat with accommodation fore and aft.

19 Some of Albert Wood's boatmen and boat horses photographed in May 1912 at the Peak Forest Wharf of Ducie Street Basin, Manchester, headquarters of the Rochdale Canal Company. Albert Wood continued trading until 1919. Both this and the previous photographs come from the collection of Reginald Wood, seen as a child sitting between the two ladies near the stern of *Bedford* in Plate 18.

20

21

20 The Rochdale Canal Company started trading in its own right in the 1880s, continuing through until July 1921. This is the final bale of the last load of cotton brought by *Primrose* to Lock Hill Mill, Sowerby Bridge, a month before the carrying fleet was disbanded. The horse is fully harnessed and ready to leave as soon as this bale is unloaded and the photographer has left. The date was 3 June 1921. These craft were designed to take 80-90 tons of cargo on a 5 feet draft, but few canals could provide this. The Rochdale Canal was hardly ever over 4 feet in depth during the early part of this century, so the maximum cargo carried would only be around 40 tons. The tonnage on this canal reached the staggering total of just under a million tons in the year 1845, just before the coming of real railway competition. A lot of this, however, was short haul traffic off the Bridgewater Canal.

21 The Rochdale Company gave their boats the names of flowers or girls. They were gaily painted in a red, white and pale blue livery. The hawse ports were called eyes, and continuing the analogy of a face, the rubbing strakes below were called whiskers. In this case the boat has been unloaded, the hatchboards have been refitted, covering the cargo hold, and the hatch cloths would normally be secured by battens, wedges and lashings. The stacked hatch boards are clearly seen on the boat behind and there are others on the wharf to the left.

22 *Emily* was one of the Calder and Hebble style keels or 'west country' boats operated by the Rochdale Canal Company and is seen here near Mirfield. Such boats were usually crewed by two people, who worked the boat itself. The third member was a horse marine, who was hired along with the horse. In this case the captain was one James Shaw, while the mate was Arthur Shaw. The horse marine was A. Wainhouse. The name of the horse is not recorded but it had the number 175. The last complete run over the full length of the canal was in 1937, and navigation was abandoned in 1952. Somehow the Rochdale Canal remained independent and was not nationalised in 1948, and while it received no income from tolls from passing boats, it was able to continue as a property company. Dale Street basin was filled in and used as a car park which provided a useful revenue also, although this area is now scheduled for redevelopment. The canal is open again from Castlefield Junction with the Bridgewater Canal through the heart of Manchester to Ducie Street Junction with the Ashton Canal and is part of the popular cruising route 'The Cheshire Ring'. The Ducie Street to Sowerby Bridge section of the canal is being worked on by a group of enthusiasts, with the help of the Government Job Creation Scheme, and eventually it is hoped to re-open it right through, although this will be an expensive business, due to alterations which have taken place to the canal bed with road widening, etc.

23

TESTIN FIR GROVE BRIDGE
MILNROW

24

TESTING FIR GROVE BRIDGE
MILNROW

23 and **24** An unusual aspect of canal maintenance — bridge testing after rebuilding on the Rochdale Canal. As many motorists know to their cost, a lot of canal bridges are hump backed, the reason for this being that the engineers, when building the canal, saved money by skimping with the length of the embankments leading up to the bridge on either side. Some canal Acts specified a length for these in order to eliminate or lessen the hump. In 1906 Firgrove Bridge, narrow, cobbled and humped, had been replaced by a wider and more easily graded structure. Before opening it for traffic the engineers are submitting it to tests, using two traction engines as a moveable load.

25 The annual outing of the local church, Sunday School or other similar group was often photographed and presumably prints sold or given to the participants. To many children this annual 'treat' would be the highlight of the year. Sometimes it took the form of a journey in horse drawn vehicles; other photographs show the people in carts behind traction engines. Where a canal passed through the neighbourhood, it was not unusual for a trading boat to be taken over for a day. Benches and people would be substituted for cargo. This is a Calder and Hebble size keel, or West Country boat, with the Littleborough Parish Church school outing around 1910, on the Rochdale Canal. The photographer has caught a miscreant throwing stones into the canal to splash the occupants.

26 Canal companies have always been very jealous of their water supplies. When canals of different companies joined, they usually insisted upon a stop lock being built, although in the majority of cases there was only a slight difference in the levels. Such a lock would prevent one company, in the event of a burst, drawing water from the other, or just letting its water level fall, and recouping from the opposition. Often the lock was in favour of the older canal which then gained a shallow lock full of water with each boat. Usually the stop lock was supervised by two men, one employed by each company; the gates were kept shut and only opened for the passage of craft. At Kings Norton junction, a pair of guillotine gates were installed near the junction of the Stratford-upon-Avon Canal and the Worcester & Birmingham Canal. Guillotine gates were used as they held back the water either side of the lock and it did not matter which of the canals had the higher level at any one time. Here, in the 1920s, the Kings Norton Lock is in full working order and the counter balance weight is clearly shown. Though these gates still survive, they are retained purely as an industrial relic.

-EBORO' PARISH CHURCH SCHOOL ANNUAL TRIP 'ON THE VOYAGE'

27 and **28** The Stratford-upon-Avon Canal is now divided into two parts. The northern section to Lapworth (Kingswood Junction) has never officially closed, but the Great Western Railway stopped navigation on it for some five years by repairing Lifford Bridge in such a way that it could not be opened by boatmen. Canal enthusiasts owe a great debt of gratitude to the work done by the Inland Waterways Association, founded in 1946 by Robert Aickman. In 1947 Lord Methuen asked a question in the House of Lords about the fixing of Lifford Bridge and was told that the bridge 'would be lifted at any time on notice of intending passage being given.' Tom Rolt, first General Secretary of the Inland Waterways Association, gave notice of intent to navigate the canal in his narrow boat *Cressy*, adding that he wished to pass under the bridge on 20 May 1947. The Great Western Railway provided a narrow boat to go ahead to clear the way in case of trouble with the derelict waterway. This boat, however, got stuck and *Cressy* was on her own. With much bow-hauling and effort *Cressy* got through to the bridge, which the railway gangers had lifted with jacks and rested on baulks of timber.

28

29 Once the principle had been established, it was essential for other boats to use the canal as often as possible or the bridge would be closed again. In 1948 Eric de Maré visited the northern section of the Stratford Canal in a converted army pontoon. As requested, he gave notice of intent to navigate. He was given an escort in the form of this old iron horse-drawn ice-breaker which preceded his boat, making a form of channel through the weed. The man in the picture also gave him help on the Lapworth flight of locks. Because of these and other pioneering cruises the northern Stratford was saved. The Warwickshire County Council, however, appealed for a warrant of abandonment for the southern section of the canal from Kingswood junction to Stratford-upon-Avon in 1958. They were thwarted by the efforts of the Stratford Canal Club and the Inland Waterways Association. The canal was offered to the National Trust, who estimated that it would cost £42,000 to restore. They raised the money and restoration under the full-time control of David Hutchings started in 1961. On 11 July 1964 the canal was finally re-opened to Stratford-upon-Avon.

30 Trade on the section from Kingswood Junction to Stratford-upon-Avon, opened in 1816, gradually declined in the twentieth century, and the section was unfit for traffic by 1940. Temple Thurston took this charming picture of one of the picturesque barrel-roofed lock houses when he travelled the canal. In his well-known book *Flower of Gloster*, first published in 1911, he comments on the traffic

. . . sometimes, they tell me, a barge makes its solitary way down to Stratford, but the locks have in the crevices of their gates all that luxuriant growth of waterweed which shows you how seldom they are used. . . .

This lock cottage is at Lowsonford; the scene has changed very little and is still a popular one with photographers.

31 Some 5½ miles above Stratford is the largest single engineering work on the lower part of the canal, the Edstone or Bearley aqueduct. In the history books this is quite overshadowed by the Pontcysyllte. Nevertheless it is one of the largest cast-iron aqueducts of its type in the country, its total length being 475 feet; it stands 28 feet above the valley at the highest point. The valley contains a road, a stream, and two railway lines. This photograph shows the structure in apparently good repair and full of water in the mid 1920s. Like the pioneer iron aqueduct at Longdon-on-Tern the towing path is constructed alongside the waterway and not over it, as at Pontcysyllte. The car owner's appreciation of good engineering is shown by his choice of vehicle, a 21 hp Lanchester of about 1924.

32 The canal came under the control of the railway in 1856; when it later came under the wing of the GWR they incorporated an unusual means of watering their locomotives. Instead of the traditional watertower or water crane, locomotives using the Alcester branch could stop under the aqueduct and draw water direct from it. The valve controlling the flow is at the bottom of the down pipe. They had a stove mounted under it to stop the pipe freezing up in mid-winter. This photograph was taken after the branch was closed.

33   The Stratford Canal was part of a larger waterway system which included the Warwickshire Avon River. In this way trade from the River Severn at Tewkesbury gained access inland to Stratford-upon-Avon itself. The last boat to use the river between Evesham and Stratford is reputed to have traded in 1873; it belonged to the firm of Spraggs of Evesham. This photograph of Lucy's Lock, the first below Stratford, is thought to have been taken around 1900. As originally constructed, Lucy's Lock had a single chamber with a fall of five feet. The water below the lock was retained by a navigation staunch about ¾ mile further on at a place called Weir Break, now the site of the Upper Avon Navigation Trust's new Weir Break lock. At a later stage the navigation staunch at Weir Break was removed and a second chamber was added at the tail of Lucy's Lock, so that it formed a staircase with a total fall of seven feet four inches. Through the efforts of the Upper Avon Navigation Trust boats can again reach Stratford from Evesham.

4   The Avon between Evesham and Tewkesbury is now known as the Lower Avon. This, too, has recently been restored to full navigation by the Lower Avon Navigation Trust. De Salis in his travels passed along this stretch of river in 1896 in his steam launch *Dragon Fly*. She was 59 feet long, and had a 6 feet 8 inch beam — an ideal size for navigating the majority of the canals of this country. Here *Dragon Fly* is seen tied up to the top gates of Wyre Lock just above Pershore.

35 One of the features of the River Avon was the watergates. This is Cropthorne watergate near Fladbury, photographed by de Salis in 1896. *Dragon Fly* can just be seen nestling against the gate. Here a lock gate is situated in a weir, and for de Salis to proceed upstream the whole of the next reach must be lowered before the gate can be opened. This was often a lengthy process — one lock could take several hours to operate. One would have thought that by the turn of this century such locks would have been done away with, but de Salis writing in Bradshaw in 1904 notes 'there are at present 33 navigation weirs or staunches in existence in England, of which 27 termed staunches are situated in the Fen country or on its tributary rivers — the other 6, which are termed weirs, consist of 4 on the Thames between Oxford and Lechlade, and 2 on the Lower Avon navigation (Warwickshire) between Tewkesbury and Evesham'. In 1961 Cropthorne watergate was destroyed in the course of making the Avon navigable once more.

36 'A navigable canal from Birmingham into the county of Warwick to the canal at Aldersley near Wolverhampton in the county of Stafford with a collateral cut to the coalmines at Wednesbury'. This was the description of the original line of the first part of the Birmingham Canal Navigations. The first stretch to be built from the coalfields of Wednesbury to the BCN Company's own wharf on Suffolk Street was completed on 6 November 1769. The full section of the main line opened on 21 September 1772. The offices of the BCN were situated opposite Paradise Street and behind this impressive frontage were two wharves. These two wharves led off from the area we now call Gas Street Basin. The offices were built in 1773 and demolished in 1913. Later the wharves were drained and filled in. From 1913 to 1939 the BCN had its offices in Daimler House, Suffolk Street, after which time they moved to Sneyd, near Walsall.

37 Here we see coal-laden day boats at the rear of the BCN offices round about 1910. While the BCN had plenty of private traders operating over its waterways the company itself traded vigorously, buying coal from the pits, transporting it, selling it, and even distributing it from the wharves by horse and cart. Difference in freeboard between the loaded and nearly empty boats is clearly shown in this photograph. Note also the anti-theft design of the cabin doors. The slide slid under the guides so that it could not be lifted. There is also a lockable bar across the rear doors.

35

38 The original plan had been for the canal to end at Newhall but this section was built a few years later. The company's headquarters wharf was used for coal traffic and the Newhall wharf for merchandise, àlso for stone and timber. The present day holiday-maker often pauses at the top of Farmer's Bridge flight of locks to spend time in the Long Boat public house. The basin outside the pub is all that is now left of the entrance to the Newhall Canal. In this photograph, taken in 1946 two years before the Newhall section of the canal was closed, we see a group of Fellows, Morton and Clayton boats moored at Cambrian Wharf with the Newhall Canal leading away in the distance. The nearest boat has been built with a small bow cabin where one or two children could have slept. On the left are the Farmer's Bridge locks with a toll keeper's office in the foreground.

39 The Birmingham main line was surveyed and built by James Brindley, who died just a few days after its completion. In true Brindley style it was a contour canal, and at one stage it meandered round Coseley Hill to avoid tunnelling. Later in 1832 the hill was tunnelled through. The only part of this meandering now in use is the section from Deepfields Junction to the British Waterways Board's maintenance yards at Bradley. One of the undertakings served by the section of the canal which has now been filled in was W. Millington and Company's Summer Hill Iron Works. Here we see a number of day boats owned by the Millington Company bringing coal in.

40 This splendid photograph of Bessanna's Basin, Old Hill, was taken in 1918, and shows how coal from Haden's Hill Colliery was brought to the wharf and transhipped. The trams or waggons are not tipper trucks, and have to be physically turned on their side for the coal to be removed. There are no mechanical aids here whatsoever; the coal is all being transhipped by hand. On average it would have taken two men about half a day to load a boat of 25 tons' capacity. In the foreground can be seen a two-handled scoop and a rake. It is generally thought that there was so much traffic from this wharf at this time that some loading had to be undertaken after dark, hence the electric lighting. Many of the Birmingham day boats were pointed at each end and could therefore hang the helm, or 'ellum, at bow or stern. The helm was always taken in board when moored to prevent damage. It was easier to hang in place when resting on the beam.

38

41

42

CANAL TUNNEL, DUDLEY CASTLE GROUNDS.

1 This well known picture from the 920s typifies a busy canal arm to a arge industrial works. There were undreds of such wharves all over the West Midlands. This arm, now filled n, served Alfred Hickman's Spring ale Furnaces at Bilston. The open ay boats brought in coke which was nloaded on the right, the corrugated ron shelters giving some protection to he men working on the wharfside. he irregular shape of the day boats is nteresting — they had a very hard ife. No great care was ever taken by heir steerers, and they were banged nto many obstructions — including ach other. Surprisingly they seem to ave had a life of up to 50 years. On he left, bars of pig iron are stacked waiting shipment away from the vharf. Possibly the picture was taken n a Sunday as there are very few eople in sight. Spring Vale Furnaces vere unusual in the Black Country in aving a series of nicknames — they vere variously known as "The 'ell oles", "the 'ot 'oles" or just "ickmans". The furnaces were no ore hot or hellish than any other; the ames may have come from Hell Lane earby. 'Hotholer' was also the name iven to some open iron or steel day

boats used for ironworks traffic, so called because of the furnaces. The last of these furnaces was demolished in 1959. The site is now occupied by a modern plant and all traces of the furnaces and the canal basin have disappeared.

42 The Earl of Dudley owned a number of coalmines, some of which were in the area of Pensnett Chase. To serve these, the Pensnett Canal was built in 1840. This short canal connected with the Dudley No 1 line at the top of Parkhead locks. Coal from the mines was brought to Wallows Basin by standard-gauge mineral railway; there loads were transhipped into the canal boats. This photograph, taken in 1927, shows the distinctive privately owned waggons (ED) unloading into typical BCN day boats. The wharf crane is a very fine example. The Pensnett Canal fell into disuse in the early 1940s, although a short section survived until 1950 before it was finally abandoned.

43 The Dudley Tunnel is the longest canal tunnel still usable in this country. Finished in 1792, it is 3154 yards long. Part of it is unlined and

hewn through solid rock. It was a very small-bore tunnel, which meant that boats could not pass in it, hence they were allowed through on a timetable. The tunnel carried a great deal of trade in its day; for example, in 1853 41,704 boats passed through — ten for every hour of the day, which is good going as they all had to be legged. In 1858 Netherton Tunnel was built some miles away but parallel, and this took a lot of the Dudley traffic. Interesting features of the tunnel were branches leading away from the main bore to serve mines or quarries. The most famous of these was the 1,227 yard side tunnel to Wrens Nest basin. Limestone mined from this point was taken out to be burnt in lime kilns alongside the canal and on the nearby Lord Ward's canal. This photograph of 1905 shows the canal to the Wrens Nest, leading out of Castle Mill basin. The chains on the wall were for boatmen to hang on to, while the boards stacked on the right are stop boards for inserting into the tunnel mouth, should it be necessary to drain the tunnel.

44   In 1950 the last commercial boat passed through the tunnel, and in 1962 the canal was officially abandoned. Thanks to the efforts of the Dudley Tunnel Preservation Society (now the Dudley Canal Trust) the tunnel has been repaired and was re-opened in 1973. Lime from the quarries in the tunnel and elsewhere came to these kilns on Lord Ward's Canal. They were built in 1842 and as can be seen boats can be brought right up to their base. It is thought that the structure on top of the kilns is a steam powered crane used for charging the kilns. The structure in the foreground is a screw elevator and grader which was used to load both boats and wagons. These kilns and part of the screw elevator structure form a major feature of the Black Country Museum, an open air museum which now occupies this site.

Black Country Lime Works.

45

45   One of the principal reasons for the building of Birmingham's canals was to carry coal from the pits to the new industry. It was also coal which caused a number of closures. Here near Leacroft Wharf on the Cannock Extension Canal the pit-heads of the Hednesford collieries can be seen, but in the foreground the maintenance gangs are rebuilding the canal walls which have been badly affected by mining subsidence from the collieries behind. The date is 1934. The simple construction of the day boat can be seen, particularly the exposed knees, very similar to those on the original boats used on the underground tunnels of the Worsley Canal system. Wooden knees were used originally but with the advent of mechanical unloading devices the coal grabs tended to inflict severe damage on the knees, so they were replaced by steel ones.

46 Mining subsidence has always been a problem on canals in Birmingham and the surrounding areas. In order to shorten the route between Dudley No 1 and 2 lines near Round Oak, a new cut three furlongs long was built in 1858 and called 'the Two Lock Line'. This short cut saved about three miles on a journey. By 1894 part of the Dudley Canal, as well as the Two Lock Line, was affected by subsidence. The subsidence was dramatic indeed, for overnight part of the canal collapsed into a mineshaft. Further subsidence took place in later years and the Two Lock Line was finally closed in March 1909. This photograph shows the Two Lock Line drained immediately after closure. The damage to the walling is very clear.

47 So worried were the BCN about the possible breaching of the canal by mining subsidence that they erected safety gates at various places. These safety gates at Northwood on the Cannock Extension Canal are seen in the process of repair in 1934. There are two pairs of gates under this bridge, mitred in each direction. Should the canal be breached the movement of the water would automatically close the gates, so preventing the canal from draining. Mining subsidence so affected the Cannock Extension Canal that commercial traffic ceased in 1961; most of it was abandoned three years later. In 1960 part of the canal sunk 21 feet, due to open cast mining nearby!

NO THROUGH ROUTE

Quite a number of canals were constructed to large towns and cities and went no further. On investigation it is surprising how many were planned to go on to somewhere else, usually linking with another canal or river to give a through route and a better chance of trade. Basingstoke always seemed a strange place for the terminus of a canal, but such a waterway could be understood if it had gone on to Southampton, as planned. Had the Grand Western stretched from Taunton to the River Exe it would have made sense, but Tiverton seems rather an insignificant place at which to end a major waterway; when one realises it was only intended to be a branch of the main line it begins to take on a new light.

Another problem with the dead-end canal was that if there was a serious blockage for any reason a great stretch of it would be cut off for long periods, having no other exit. The Cromford suffered this fate when mining subsidence affected Butterley tunnel. Other canals in this category closed for all the usual reasons; lack of water, or lack of trade or, as so often happened, being bought by a railway company who took no interest in them or closed them down immediately and built over the bed, so gaining easy access to good routes. The North Staffordshire Railway's route along the narrow Churnet Valley, which replaced the extension of the Caldon Canal from Froghall to Uttoxeter in 1846, is an example of this.

48

48 One of the most difficult canals to comprehend is the Basingstoke. It leaves the River Wey Navigation at New Haw near Weybridge, and journeys 37 miles through Surrey and Hampshire to Basingstoke. Why Basingstoke, which is only now, with London overspill, becoming a town of any real size? The canal came into being as part of the dream of linking ports such as Southampton, Portsmouth and Bristol with London. It was opened in 1794, but before this date there were plans for it to be connected with both the Andover Canal and the Itchen Navigation at Winchester, so linking London with Southampton by inland waterway. None of this came to pass, so the canal had to make do with traffic to and from Basingstoke and the places *en route*. One of the chief exports from Basingstoke town was timber. This general view of Basingstoke wharf is thought to have been taken in 1905 when the canal was still just navigable. Two boats can be seen moored along the side of E.C. White & Son's timber yard.

49 This photograph shows the yard in close-up and is thought to have been taken approximately five years later. It is interesting to note that Whites' business was established two years before the canal was actually opened.

50 By 1825 the canal was already falling into decay and for the rest of its life it had a continual struggle to remain solvent. This photograph of Broadwater, near Basing, was taken in 1905. This stretch was still officially navigable at the time, although the weed in the water would make the passage of craft difficult. The walls on the canal bank in the distance are those of Basing House. It is said that while the canal was being built around the house 800 golden guineas were discovered. These were reputedly part of Oliver Cromwell's treasure, said to have been hidden somewhere in the grounds. Broadwater was a local beauty spot, and the well-used tow path has been trodden by walkers rather than the hooves of boat horses.

51 The most celebrated voyage on the canal must have been that of A.J. Harmsworth in his narrow boat *Basingstoke* in which he tried to navigate to the town of Basingstoke during the last few months of 1913. The Canal's Act of 1778 had a clause in it which stated that 'Should the canal be disused for the space of five years, the land should be reconveyed to the previous owners. . . .' As the last recorded voyage to Basingstoke town had been in 1910, Harmsworth thought he ought to try and get through, to keep the canal open for himself and other traders. On November 16 1913 *Basingstoke* left Ash Vale loaded with a token cargo of sand. One of the first major obstacles was Greywell tunnel (1,230 yards long) which had partially collapsed in 1890 but had been repaired. In this photograph the crew are shafting the boat into the tunnel but, as can be seen, a cross plank has been positioned to allow two people to lie on their backs and leg or walk the boat through the tunnel. The substantial windlass is there to help extract the boat when hard aground.

52 Early in December the boat was struggling among the reeds (bottom photograph) near Mapledurwell, 4½ miles from its objective. It was being towed at this time by one horse and at least eight men. The following account was written by *Daily Express* reporter Ivor Heald.

Little did I think when I sailed away from Mapledurwell last evening, singing shanties and waving handkerchiefs, that in a few short hours our ship would be coming back that way again, stern foremost. Alas! The canal had another bad puncture during the night, and at dawn the look-out discovered that we were running directly on a mile of dry land. One of the narrowest escapes we have had. The captain, with admirable presence of mind, immediately orders us to reverse the horse, and we ran back about half a mile for safety. . . .'

Mr Heald's report makes the whole episode sound like something from a children's adventure story book. It is thought that the voyage ended at Basing and that the boat did not get through to Basingstoke. Even so the canal was not closed on this occasion but sold.

53 This scene was taken at Crookham around 1904, when the Basingstoke Canal had been put up for sale. It is thought that the narrow boat (Lot 124) was the canal company's work boat used for canal maintenance. Previously this boat had been a trading boat which was then bought by A.J. Harmsworth and converted into a simple house boat. From 1890 he lived on it with his wife before selling it in 1895 to the canal company who converted it back again. By the time this picture was taken it can be seen to be in very poor condition. Some would call it a 'watercress bed', the boatman's term for a leaky boat.

53

54 Pontoon Building, Aldershot.

55

The Canal with Royal Engineers Yard.

54 and 55 The government confirmed in 1854 that it was going to build a military camp at Aldershot. Previous to this, the common land in the area had been earmarked for troop training. With the building of the camp over the next five years a great deal of extra trade was brought to the Basingstoke Canal in the form of building materials, so much so that the tonnages coming on to the canal from the River Wey increased from 10,669 in 1854 to 19,720 the following year and to a staggering 27,664 tons in 1856. The coming of the camp helped save the ailing canal. The presence of some 15,000 troops brought trade in the form of army supplies, hundreds of tons of oats for the horses and sometimes even a backload of horse manure. The army also used the canal for training and manoeuvres, as these two photographs clearly show. Bridge building was one of the specialities of the Royal Engineers who were stationed there and the canal has seen many temporary structures built across it during exercises. The temporary pontoon is obviously based on barrels, while in the other photograph the two craft are proper bridge pontoons. The pictures are thought to have been taken around 1910.

56 This photograph shows two boats at the fifty yard Little Tunnel on the top part of the Basingstoke Canal, above the longer tunnel at Greywell. The photograph was probably taken in 1904 or 1905 and is believed to show the narrow boats *Maudie* and *Ada* belonging to the Hampshire Brick and Tile Company of Nateley. The boats are moored and a gang plank has been put ashore. As there was no wharf at this point it may be that the horse had been taken down the lane which crosses the tunnel to the nearby farrier for the fitting of new shoes. It is thought that the boats were built initially for the Surrey and Hampshire Canal Company around 1880 before passing into the hands of the brickworks. A number of their boats were built at Appledore in North Devon and brought round to Bristol, lashed to the side of coastal vessels, thence via the Kennet and Avon Canal and River Thames. These boats are typical of craft trading on that canal, which frequently went onto the River Thames. Most of them had their bows built up with wash boards; these would help stop heavily laden craft from shipping water on windy reaches of the tideway, or protect them from the wash from tugs pulling them. Incidentally, they were always breasted up when on the tideway. The boats are both fitted with a small windlass on the fore end, for an anchor when working on the Thames. Note the absence of a water can on the cabin roof. Instead one boat has a water barrel, a custom more familiar on boats in the North of England but common on the Basingstoke. The traditional roses and castles come on visiting boats only; the Harmsworth family did not like them.

7 Not much is known about boat building on the Basingstoke Canal prior to 1918. It is known that A.J. Harmsworth started repairing boats at Ash Vale around 1902, and in 1918 he built the barge *Rosaline*. Soon he was building boats at approximately yearly intervals. They were constructed to his own design, based on his experience of trading on the Basingstoke Canal, the River Wey Navigation and the River Thames. The barges were 73 feet long and 13 feet 10½ inches wide, designed to carry up to 80 tons each. The pictures show the barge *Aldershot* under construction in 1932. The use of the boatbuilder's adze can be clearly seen. Although a corrugated iron shed had been built in 1925 to enable such building work to be carried out under cover, it was not in use at this time. After launching, the barges were taken across the canal to the boat repair yard where they were fitted out. It is estimated that it took four to six men 3½ months to build a barge and the cost of the *Aldershot* in 1932 was £900. The last barge was built in 1935 though repair work continued until 1947.

58 While this may be a well-known photograph it does give a good indication of the primitive methods employed when repairs were necessary on the waterways. This picture was taken as late as 1912, yet there is no sign whatsoever of mechanisation. These were the methods and the tools used for canal construction 140 or so years before. Forks, spades and shovels are used for digging while the spoil is carried away in wheelbarrows over precariously constructed 'barrow runs' to a suitable dumping ground. Some of the more important lock gates on the canal were made in oak rather than pitch pine because oak was more durable. The Harmsworth family carried out repair works on the canal before they became the owners, this work being done in lieu of tolls. The white gates here on Goldsworth IX near Woking on the Basingstoke Canal came about after a careless workman spilt white paint over part of a new gate while under construction. He was therefore instructed to paint the whole gate white. In recent times the canal to Greywell has been jointly purchased by the Surrey and Hampshire County Councils and is being actively restored by them in conjunction with Surrey and Hampshire Canal Society.

59 Many people think that pleasure boating is a relatively new pastime on the canals. However, the day hire of boats such as punts, canoes or rowing boats has been going on for many years. In 1883, for example, there were ten boat stations on the Basingstoke Canal. The one near the army camps at Ash Vale was perhaps the best known. Long-distance pleasure trips such as that described in Temple Thurston's *Flower of Gloster* were not, of course, very common. This scene shows Frimley top lock around the turn of the century. The building is the canal company's carpentry shop and blacksmith's forge. Moored outside is a steam boat with cabin, possibly used by the canal's directors; it appears in other photographs of this area, though Frimley was no doubt its home mooring. The smaller steam launch appears to be a visitor. Could it possibly be connected with the tent on the lockside?

60 In order that coastal vessels should not have to navigate around Lands End to reach the Bristol Channel from the English Channel, an ambitious canal, known as the Grand Western Canal, was projected to run from Topsham on the River Exe in Devon to Taunton in Somerset. The first survey was made in 1792 but work did not start until 1810. The first section to be made was a level pound of 11 miles from Tiverton to Holcombe. This section was one of the three branches envisaged for the main line. It was believed that this would be an easy section to make, and that there would be considerable traffic in limestone over it from Westleigh quarries to Tiverton. This picture demonstrates that parts of the canal were very straight and had a good towing path. Here we see a maintenance gang cutting weed which would choke the canal and impede the passage of boats. The cutter consists of a series of blades on a long rope, which was worked back and forth in a sawing action by men on either bank, so cutting off the weed low down on the stem.

61 As the Channel linking project faded away, it became imperative that the canal should be connected to Taunton to allow cargo to flow to Tiverton from the Bristol Channel via the Bridgwater and Taunton Canal. A tub boat canal with lifts and inclined planes was built to Taunton. The mechanics of the lifts and planes caused some trouble but more significant still, a branch railway was built to Tiverton in 1848. Within a year the through haul tonnage from Taunton to Tiverton dropped from 10,532 to 2,456 tons. In 1856 the Great Western Railway bought the canal, closing the tub boat section eleven years later. The remaining section (the original 11 miles) carried a small amount of trade up until 1924. This amounted to a few boats; de Salis in Bradshaw says two, but this picture shows three and another photograph from the same series also shows three that were engaged in roadstone and limestone traffic. Here we see them being loaded at the quarries near Loudwell at Whipcott wharf, about 1900. The boats could load 8-10 tons each. The canal horses are standing by to haul the load towards Tiverton.

61

Even though latterly the Grand Western Canal only carried a few thousand tons of goods a year, the Great Western Railway had to keep in reasonable repair. A series of leaks at Halberton caused problems in the 1890s. By the end of 1905 the receipts for 6 months trading were reputed to have been £119. By the same token expenses had not been very high either at £197. Perhaps there had been no item of major repair in the months covered by the figures. This photograph, taken on 27 April 1921 near Sellake Bridge, shows that the water has drained out through the bed of the canal, leaving behind it a gaping fissure and the threat of a bank collapse. It is surprising that repairs of this magnitude were justified at this time and that a breach such as this did not close the canal for good, as it was only three years before its final closure. This section of the canal gave continual trouble through leakage.

63 Here workmen are digging out the clay bed and replacing it with new puddle in an attempt to stop some of the water loss. Again, this photograph was taken in April 1921 and near the previous location. After closure of the canal this portion was dry for many years. In recent years when the canal was being repaired, it was this section which caused the restorers the most trouble as it still leaked.

64 The Herefordshire and Gloucestershire Canal had a short and chequered career. It was quite a latecomer, and one would have thought that its promoters would have taken heed of the troubles of some other mainly rural ventures. In 1794 the canal was opened from the River Severn opposite Gloucester to Oxenhall a few miles from Ledbury. Here the line was held up while a 2,192 yard tunnel was cut. However, a series of small coalmines were opened in this area about the same time, and these gave some traffic through to the River Severn. In 1798 the tunnel was completed and the waterway reached Ledbury. This picture is one of the few photographs remaining of the canal before its eventual closure. This is Oxenhall Lock; the date is thought to be 1880.

65

5   The effect the waterway had on
Ledbury was very marked.
Priestley's *Navigable Rivers and
Canals* says

. the opening of Oxenhall tunnel
effected an immediate reduction in
the price of coals at Ledbury of no
less than ten shillings and sixpence
per ton; that quantity being sold for
thirteen shillings and sixpence
when, before the opening of the
navigation, twenty-four shillings was
the price. Nor is it with the
coalmines alone that this canal opens
a ready communication; limestone,
iron, lead, and other productions of
South Wales, as well as those of the
immediate neighbourhood of
Hereford, may, by means of this
canal, be conveyed to London,
Bristol, Liverpool, Hull, and various
other parts of the kingdom, entirely
by water carriage.

This traffic was not enough and in
1840 (42 years later) work was
started again on the section of the
canal to connect Ledbury with
Hereford. Hereford basin was
reached and opened in 1845. This
undated engraving shows a busy
scene at Hereford; timber was
obviously playing an important part
in the cargoes of the canal, but were

the boats really that design, or is it
artist's licence?

66   The Welshpool and Llanfair
Railway in mid Wales is an enigma
in railway terms. Here was a railway
being opened as late as 1903, purely
to serve a local farming community.
It was narrow-gauge, and therefore
its rolling stock could not pass on to
the main line at Welshpool. In
Welshpool it ignored the canal,
which it crosses by an iron bridge.
Nor was there any attempt to use it
as a feeder for traffic, presumably
because by then the
Montgomeryshire Canal no longer
prospered. This canal runs from
Welsh Frankton near Ellesmere
through to Welshpool and on to
Newtown. It is really an amalgam of
three canals, the first section having
been built by the Ellesmere Canal
Company to tap the rich limestone
deposits at Llanymynech. The
Eastern Branch of the
Montgomeryshire Canal proper was
built from here on to Garthmyl, and
the Western Branch from here to
Newtown. The Eastern branch was
completed in 1797, but the Western
did not follow until 1821. One of the

main structures on the route was the
Berriew aqueduct below Welshpool
on the Eastern Branch. It crosses
the River Rhiew by two 30 foot
arches, with a smaller arch at either
end. In 1889 major repairs became
necessary as can be seen here. The
canal has been stanked off in the
foreground and has a crude pump
mounted in the centre of the dam.
The canal water is being allowed to
drain off by an overflow weir on the
right to the river below. A barrow
run crosses the bed on trestles, while
mechanisation is provided by a series
of light railway lines. In the
background are some narrowboats,
probably bringing in cargoes of
bricks to help with the building
work.

67 A surprisingly high tonnage was carried considering the Montgomeryshire Canal's rural character, the highest recorded figure being 113,580 tons in 1840-1. Railways came late into the area — which helped — but they reached Welshpool and Newtown in 1861, and thenceforward trade steadily declined. One quoted figure shows it as low as 8,992 tons in 1923, which is about the date of this photograph. Here a loaded maintenance boat from the LMS Railway Company locks down at Welsh Frankton. An attempt was made to close the Western Branch as long ago as 1876, with the possible closure of all sections in 1886, but as it was making a profit it was allowed to continue. In the light of subsequent developments it seems strange that the costly repairs to the Berriew aqueduct in the previous picture should have taken place on a section of canal leading to one known to be financially unsound. The Western Branch was closed in 1936 when the canal burst at Dandyfield. Parts of the canal are now being restored by The Shropshire Union Canal Society.

68 An unusual aspect of the traffic on the Montgomeryshire Canal was a daily fly boat service for light goods and passengers from Rednal at the bottom of the Frankton flight of locks to Welshpool and Newtown. At Rednal the boat connected with trains to Chester, Birkenhead, Liverpool and Shrewsbury. You could, for example, leave Newtown at 7 am by fly boat and be in Liverpool by 4.5 pm. An unusual craft often seen on the canal was the Shropshire Union Canal Company's inspection craft, normally based at Ellesmere and photographed here at Pant. The boat was called *Inspector* by the Shropshire Union and was used by them until 1934. Unfortunately the date of the picture is not known. *Inspector* was purchased in 1934 by a Mr Hobson-Greenwood who said that she was 'fitted out in a grand style with a long saloon and a mahogany table with drop leaves which ran the whole length of the saloon . . . the cutlery, china and cut glass were the finest and were all marked "Shropshire Union Canal Company".'

69 The Shropshire Union Canal Carrying Company was controlled by the London and North Western Railway and unlike most railway controlled companies it tried to make its canal carrying pay. By the early 1900s they had over 400 boats trading. In 1921 the Railway Unions, completely oblivious to the requirements of canal carrying, insisted that the boatmen and their families should only work an eight-hour day as did the railmen. This was the last straw, and as the fleet was not paying its way it was disbanded and the boats broken up or sold to smaller traders. The Rochdale and Leeds and Liverpool Companies gave up their carrying fleets at the same time for the same reasons. Between the locks at Welsh Frankton was the boat-building yard of Henry Egerton who later passed it on to John Beech. This yard served the needs of the smaller traders. S. Owen & Son were typical. They owned this one boat and traded from a wharf at Pant near Llanymynech. In this picture their boat *Five Sisters* has just been repainted at the boat yard. John Beech is standing in the cabin.

John Beech also owned a couple of boats himself and traded along the length of the canal. He is seen here standing with his family on his own boat *Olga*.

1 Another person who spent a lot of time cruising for pleasure on the canals in the 1930s was Captain J. Carr-Ellison, who, in May 1930, piloted a 12 foot open motor launch from London to Ripon in thirteen days! In 1933 a chance meeting with another enthusiast, a Mr Anglin, at Worcester, introduced him to the idea of converting a working narrow boat for cruising. Thus in 1935 Captain Carr-Ellison commissioned Salters of Oxford to make him a floating home suitable for long distance cruising. The basis for his craft was a horsedrawn working boat into which was grafted a Coventry Victor engine which normally resided in a van used during the winter months on the owner's Northumberland estate. Another import from the estates was a mare called 'Doll' who was kept in readiness if ever they were to explore waterways known to be clogged with weed. The Carr-Ellisons travelled widely. One such trip was over the

Montgomeryshire Canal and they are seen here climbing through the locks at Welsh Frankton shortly before the canal was finally breached.

72 The canals of Shropshire are extremely complicated and difficult to understand. They came into being as a result of the explosion of industry in the area now known as Telford — made up of such towns as Wellington, Oakengates, Donnington, Dawley, Madeley and the most famous of all to the industrial archaeologist, Coalbrookdale. The Shrewsbury Canal was opened in 1797 to bring coal from the Oakengates area to the town of Shrewsbury. Later in life this canal was joined at Wappenshall by the Newport branch of the Birmingham and Liverpool Junction Canal, completed in 1835. This at last gave all the products of the area ready access to the Midland canal system. The Shrewsbury and surrounding canals were built initially to take tub boats because the waterway involved a number of inclined planes. These were necessary in this case because of the hilly terrain and a lack of good water supply. This picture is thought to have been taken in 1907 and shows

the actions of a typical man-and-wife team as they bring their horse-drawn boat into the lock at Newport. The horse has already started feeding from his nosebag, the man has just checked the forward motion of the boat with the fore end strap around the strapping post, while the wife has jumped off and is about to close the top gate.

Canal Lock, Newport Salop

73 Josiah Clowes was the engineer initially responsible for the Shrewsbury Canal. One of the problems to be overcome in the making of the canal was the crossing of the River Tern at Longdon, some 16 feet above the level of the surrounding meadows. Clowes built out earth embankments and constructed a masonry aqueduct. While the canal was still being built, serious flooding occurred in 1795, washing this structure away. Clowes died soon afterwards and Telford took over. Using the original stone abutments he built a cast-iron trough 62 yards long by 7 feet 6 inches wide and 4 feet 6 inches deep. The cast iron plates were made nearby in the works of William Reynolds, famous ironmasters of Ketley. Reynolds is thought to have had a hand in the design. The tow path takes the form of a narrower trough alongside. This was the first major cast-iron aqueduct in the country and pre-dated the Pontcysyllte by 9 years. Telford was appointed engineer for the Shrewsbury Canal on 28 February 1795 and produced his plans for this aqueduct soon afterwards. The use of iron for Pontcysyllte was officially approved in July 1795, so it can be seen that Longdon on Tern was a trial for the larger structure. The photograph was taken in 1963 when there was still some water in it, but later the water was drained and the bed of the canal and the aqueduct used as a farm track.

74 The Berwick Tunnel is one of the features of the Shrewsbury Canal. Priestley says 'the tunnel near Atcham is also remarkable; it is nine hundred and seventy yards in length and 10 feet wide, with a towing path 3 feet wide, constructed of wood, and supported on bearers from the wall.' This picture of the Shrewsbury end of the tunnel is thought to have been taken in the 1880s. A tub boat can be seen in the tunnel mouth. The tow path was removed in 1819. Bradshaw in 1904 adds a novel twist.

There are no fixed hours for boats to pass through this tunnel. There is a white mark in the middle of the tunnel, and should two boats meet, the one who has reached the middle of the tunnel

first has the right of way.

The author can appreciate the position of two boats meeting in the centre and neither wanting to give way. It happened to him one evening in the middle of the 1¾ mile Harecastle Tunnel. A similar story is told of Greywell tunnel on the Basingstoke Canal when two boats met in the centre:

. . . neither of the captains would give way. The owner of one barge, a miller, near Odiham, sent in a boat with provisions and beer for his men, and so starved their opponents into surrender.

75 and **76**   These two photographs show the top and bottom of the Trench inclined plane, part of the Shrewsbury Canal and the last plane to work in this country; it did not close until as late as 1921. It was built and open by 1794, almost three years before the completion of the rest of the canal. Tub boats were floated onto a cradle running on lines very similar to a railway. The cradles had larger wheels at the back to compensate for the angle of the plane, and in an attempt to keep the tub boat on as even a keel as possible. They also had an extra set of wheels at the front which were mounted on the outside of the framework of the cradle. As the cradle went over the cill at the top of the plane, these wheels would engage on rails on the dockside which would stop the cradle tilting to a severe angle. The picture of the top of the plane shows an unladen tub boat which has just come over the cill into the top pound and is about to be eased off into the water. The engineer in charge of the plane at the time of the photograph (standing in the doorway) was William Jones who died in 1954 at the age of 84. He was assisted by a young brakeman (standing centre) called Frank Owen who was 88 when he died in 1963. The steam engine was required to even up the loads, as it was not always possible to have a loaded boat pull up an empty one by gravity and the power of the engine was required to pull the boats over the cill at the top. The engine was renewed in 1842 and worked through until the closure 80 years later, Frank Owen claiming that it would work all day on a steam pressure of ten pounds per square inch. He also indicated that 50-60 boats moving over the plane would be considered an average for a busy day. Traffic was mainly one-way, coal going down to the Shrewsbury Canal, but an occasional cargo such as wheat came up, for Bullocks Flour Mills at Donnington, the last traffic on the plane. The heavily laden boat moored here is thought to be loaded with materials for the maintenance work which is going on and is not the next boat to go down. The original of this photograph is undated but it was probably taken around 1900. The picture of the bottom of the plane gives some idea of the rise in relation to the surrounding countryside and also its proximity to an urban area. Again the date is uncertain but it could have been as late as 1921, when the plane was abandoned. There is no sign of a cradle on either of the two lines although all appears to be in quite good repair. The warehouse on the right would have been a transhipment points for goods which came down the plane from tub boats on to narrow boats, both of which can be seen in the basin.

77 The firm of G.F. Milnes and Co, well known as tramcar builders, opened a new factory at Hadley, near Wellington, in July, 1900. As with all such organisations, an artist's impression of the new factory was prepared before the new building was completed to enable the company to publish details of their expansion. This picture is an enlargement of just part of that impression. It shows that the factory was built close to that section of the old Shrewsbury Canal between Wappenshall and Trench, near its junction with the Newport branch. While the artist may have been accurate in his portrayal of the guillotine lock gate and the fairly typical Welsh canal type bridge, he had obviously never seen a narrow boat when he drew this picture. His version bears no relation to the size of the lock. The boats in the foreground are unloading coal into the boiler house of the factory, while the dock behind is for the import of timber, for the bodybuilding side of the business.

78 The Donnington Wood Canal was the first of the Shropshire group. Some 5 miles long and on the level, it was originally intended to give access to the Newport-Wolverhampton road. In the end it was connected by the Trench inclined plane to the Shrewsbury Canal, most of its traffic going in that direction. Very little is known about this photograph of a typical tub boat of the area. Obviously the boat is out of use and pulled up on the bank of a small stream. The caption attached to it in the original album from which it was copied says 'tub boat made Lilleshall Company Limited, Old Yard Works, which closed in 1851'. The tub boats measured 19 feet 9 inches long by 6 feet 2 inches wide. They would normally carry 5 tons of cargo on a draft of 2 feet.

79 Within Shrewsbury the terminal basin was abandoned in 1922, and in 1936 the last recorded boat berthed in the town. Three years later the canal was abandoned within the limits of the town. This photograph is of the wharf at the village of Uffington just outside Shrewsbury and was taken at about the time of the passing of the last trading boat. This photograph has a timeless quality about it, but clearly illustrates the very narrow cobbled access to the wharfside. Such access was all that was necessary for a horse and cart, though no use for to-day's articulated lorry. The wharfside crane is typical. It would have been hand operated and quite capable of lifting boxes or sacks from the holds of the boats.

80 Grantham is 20 miles due east of Nottingham. It is an important town in the midst of a mainly agricultural area. In the mid-1700s all goods coming to or from the town had to be carried overland, but in 1791 a canal from the Trent to Grantham was planned. It was completed in 1797. Priestley, writing about the canal in 1831 says

The Navigation is now complete . . . and the advantages to the town of Grantham are very great; corn, timber, coals, lime, and many other articles both of import and export, by the communication open through this canal, with those of Nottingham and Cromford, are now transferred at a comparatively easy cost, giving amongst other things, to the inhabitants of this district, the comforts of fuel at a much less expense than heretofore.

The locks on the canal were built to a width of fourteen foot which allowed both Trent craft and narrow boats to trade on it. This pair of boats is moored at a wharf just outside Grantham in 1910.

81

82

81 While coal had once been a major traffic on the waterway, by the turn of the twentieth century it was being taken by rail, so much so that total cargo carried on the canal in 1905 amounted to only 18,000 tons. 8,000 tons of this, incidentally, was manure, an unusual cargo to be found in such quantity at so late a date. By 1910, the approximate date of this picture, few trade craft disturbed the waters at Ealesfield Lane Bridge, so pleasure boating and fishing took over. The building in the centre looks to be a boat repair dock or boat house.

82 In 1833 J. Rofe and his son put forward an idea to link the Grantham Canal from its terminal basin, seen here, to the Sleaford Navigation some 16 miles away, so gaining access to Boston and the east coast trade, but finance was against it and the money could not be raised. As it was, the Grantham Canal was in trouble because of the high tolls it charged. For example, corn bound for Manchester was being taken via Newark, Selby and then by railway, which was cheaper than using water transport all the way. More surprisingly, Nottingham coal, one of the original reasons for the canal's very existence, was more expensive in Grantham than coal bought in Yorkshire, taken by sea to Gainsborough, thence by the Trent to Newark, and finally overland! Trade dwindled so much that the canal was officially abandoned in 1936. The canal warehouses seen here were demolished in October 1929. The ladies in the foreground were the Misses Cameron who ran a boat hiring business from the basin in the 1920s.

83 To gather the information for Bradshaw de Salis travelled by water over 14,000 miles in eleven years. Most of the journeys, in the southern part of England at any rate, were undertaken in his steam launch. On other occasions, such as his visits to the Cromford Canal in 1897, and here on the Grantham, he used a horsedrawn working boat. Here we see him resting on a deck chair in the hold of a working boat somewhere on the Grantham Canal. The photograph clearly shows how the upright stands are fitted within the hold with the top planks running over them. Over the top planks would be fitted the cloths covering the cargo if it was of a type which would be affected by wet weather.

84 Once a canal is abandoned it does not just disappear. Disused canals need maintenance the same as operational ones, otherwise banks will burst and floods will occur. In recent years the campaigning Inland Waterways Association have always maintained that it is cheaper to keep a canal open to navigation than to fill it in and culvert the water. This photograph was taken some time around the beginning of World War II at West Bridgford, Nottingham. It shows a lifting bridge spanning the Grantham Canal which still contained a full level of water, even though the waterway had been closed for some four years. There is now an active Grantham Canal Restoration Society.

85 Melton Mowbray is now famous for meat pies, but in the late eighteenth century it was basically a small rural community with a population of under 1,700. Despite this, it was thought desirable to give the town a waterway, and one was opened in 1797 to connect it with the Soar Navigation near Syston. The River Wreak was made navigable; in the course of its 11-mile route it rises 71 feet by means of twelve locks. Again the main cargo was to be coal. Prior to its building, the *Leicester Journal* of 29 October 1785 commented that Melton Mowbray was 'paying 18d per hundred weight for coals which a water conveyance would reduce to about 9d.' This photograph is of the basin at Melton Mowbray in Burton Street. The pub on the right hand side of the street is the Boat Inn, the only landmark associated with the basin that you will still find in Melton Mowbray. Another waterway leads out of the basin on the right side. This is the Oakham Canal, completed in 1802; it had a very short life, closing as early as 1846, after a takeover by the Midland Railway. Even in its last years traffic had not been that bad for a rural canal: 31,182 tons were carried up to Oakham. Much of this was coal, which went away overland for Stamford and the surrounding areas. 4,000 tons of agricultural produce such as grain and wool were the main exports. The craft in the photograph is one of the 70-foot-long wide boats which operated on the Upper Trent and inland as far as Leicester on the Soar Navigation.

7 The Nutbrook Canal branched
om the Erewash Canal near
andiacre in Derbyshire and
roceeded to Shipley Wharf. But the
pper part was quite unnavigable by
895, although trade on the lower
aches to the large Stanton
onworks continued until 1949;
ree years earlier the company had
ought the remains of the canal for
use as their principal supply of
water. The weedy nature of the
waterway can be seen in this
charming Victorian photograph
taken just two years after the canal
reputedly closed to navigation. The
spectacle of boys bathing in the
nude, watched by girls, goes against
many of the traditional ideas one
associates with this period!

86 With the closing of the Oakham
Canal and the coming of the
Midland Railway, Melton Mowbray
lost some of its trade. During the
1860s the canal company tried to sell
the waterway, first to the
Loughborough Navigation, and,
when this failed, to the Midland
Railway itself. As the Midland did
not see the navigation as a threat
they also declined the offer. The
canal closed on 1 August 1877. As it
was a river navigation careful
attention had to be paid to the
livelihood of all mill owners along
the route. A watermill is no use
without an adequate supply of water.
The river was weired at each mill to
provide a mill pond, making a
convenient spot for the building of a
lock. This also accounts for the large
number of locks, with an average
drop of six feet each. This
photograph of the lock at Ratcliffe-
on-the-Wreak was taken in 1906, 29
years after the canal had closed. The
lock gates have gone, but the chamber
is in good order. The side paddles
appear to be in working order, but the
level of the water in the mill pond has
been maintained by providing a dam
of almost the same height as the
previous lock gates.

88

FROGHALL.
CHURNET VALLEY.

89

Canal and Bridge, Cheddleton

CONSALL, CHURNET VALL[E]

Beside the top lock at Etruria
the Potteries a branch canal turns
[of]. At this junction there used to be
[a n]otice saying 'The Caldon Canal is
[clo]sed but craft up to two foot draft
[m]ay navigate Etruria/Hazelhurst at
[th]eir own risk.' Under it was a
[sign]epost saying 'Uttoxeter 30 miles'.
[As] the notice said the Caldon was
[na]vigable, the author tried part of it
[in] a British Waterways-owned hire
[bo]at in October 1970. It was hard
[go]ing and required the use of a crow
[ba]r to operate some of the lock
[pa]ddle gear. Two years later full
[re]storation of the waterway
[co]mmenced. The Caldon branch of
[th]e Trent and Mersey was opened in
[17]79 to Froghall to tap the very
[val]uable limestone deposits in the
[qu]arries at Caldon Low. The lime
[kil]ns, still situated at Froghall, are
[sai]d to be some of the best and
[lar]gest remaining in Staffordshire.
[Th]is picture of the wharves at
[Fr]oghall was taken in 1910. Narrow
[bo]ats are seen being loaded with
[li]mestone, one of the principle users
[be]ing the Brunner Mond Works at
[Sa]ndbach in Cheshire. Traffic to
[the]se works ceased with their closure
[in] 1920.

89 At Cheddleton, some 11 miles
from the Etruria end of the branch,
is a famous water-driven flint mill.
Some types of pottery called for
quantities of ground flints in their
making and the Cheddleton Mill,
recently restored, is one of the few
remaining. It lies behind the
buildings on the right of the
picture. The photograph shows a
horse boat heavily laden with
limestone passing the wharf at
Cheddleton; it dates from about
1910. On the left are two unusual
boats. The nearest one is an ice
breaker which would have been
towed along the canal by a team of
horses to break up the ice at times of
heavy frost. A group of men rocked
the boat from side to side as they
went, so smashing a wider channel
in the thick ice. Behind it is a
maintenance boat fitted with a fore
cabin, some form of mid-boat shelter
as well as a rear cabin, and a very
large pump mounted amidships. A
restored working narrow boat is now
on show outside the flint mill at
Cheddleton. It was the *Vienna*,
formerly with the carrying company
Fellows Morton and Clayton.

90 Above Froghall the Caldon
Canal uses just over a mile of the
River Churnet. A horse-drawn
narrow boat loaded with limestone is
seen here coming off the artificial
cut into the river at Consall. The
canal tow path crosses the river by
the bridge on the right. Under
bridge 49 in the background is a
flood lock to protect the canal from
taking too much water should the
river be in flood.

91 Narrow boat *Shannon* by Bridge 49 at Consall Forge. The flood gates are clearly shown. The boat is fully loaded with limestone and the top planks can be seen lashed to the stands. There is no cratch at the fore end, just a stand. This was common practice on northern narrow boats. The unadorned chimney was common up to the early 1900s. The brass rings so often seen these days were a fashion of number ones and became general in the 1920s. The building under the bridge is thought to be the terminus of the Consall plateway.

92 This and the following photograph are two superb pictures of the narrow boat *Dora*, belonging to Price and Son of Brierley Hill on the Dudley Canal, and are believed to be previously unpublished. Both were taken around 1900. *Dora* is seen here between Podmore's Flint Mill and Consall Forge with a cargo of limestone. The spare tow line is hanging from the cabin side close to the steerer. The round castle picture decoration on the cabin door is unusual — these are more often square. The maintenance boat in the background would appear to be an old-fashioned spoon dredger.

93 *Dora* at Consall Forge most probably on the same trip. The picture clearly shows the decoration on the helm, the special rope work and swan's neck. The number on the side of the cabin is the gauging number, possibly from the Dudley Canal. Both this and the previous picture show limestone heaped high at the fore end, also the side cloths neatly rolled along the side of the hold, there being no need to cover the cargo. This is a Midlands boat; thus it has a cratch at the fore end.

91

94

94 In 1802 the Trent and Mersey Canal Company opened a branch canal from Hazelhurst to Leek, in the process of which they tapped a very valuable water supply from Rudyard Lake, which, after it had flowed down the Caldon Canal, fed the Trent and Mersey, so providing water to both sides of the Harecastle summit. Commercial traffic to Leek had waned by the 1930s. There had been some coal traffic up to 1934 from Foxley near Stoke-on-Trent and there had also been a small amount of traffic down from Leek to Milton (Stoke-on-Trent) with tar, which lasted until 1939. After this date the canal was disused and under the LMSR Act it was abandoned, and sections within the town boundaries were filled in during the period 1961-3. This photograph, taken around 1900, shows Leek Basin with an Anderton Carrying Company boat moored under the overhanging warehouse. The wharf crane shows up clearly as does the wharfinger's house behind. In the background the water tank at Leek railway station can be seen. This is now all demolished as well.

95

OAKMOOR

95 Twenty years after the opening of the Caldon Canal an Act was granted for its extension down the Churnet Valley to Uttoxeter, hence the milepost quoting '30 miles to Uttoxeter' already mentioned. This extension, opened in 1811, was 13½ miles long and dropped down the valley by some seventeen locks. In 1846 the North Staffordshire Railway Company bought the Trent

and Mersey Canal and along with it the Caldon. The new owners immediately closed the Froghall-Uttoxeter section, and laid a railway line along it. From this it is easy to see why there are few (if any) illustrations of this section of the canal taken when it was still operating commercially. One of the purposes behind the abortive extension was to service the large

copper and brass works at Oakmoor. This typical Trent and Mersey style mile post was photographed in May of 1958 in the yard of Thomas Bolton and Sons Ltd, Oakmoor.

96 The stonework of the California Lock on the Uttoxeter Canal has survived the 133 years of neglect since it was last used, and is in a remarkably good condition.

7 and 98 Richard Arkwright was born in Preston, Lancashire, in 1732. He later became apprenticed to a barber, eventually setting up his own business as a barber and wig maker. Arkwright was interested in machinery, and in conjunction with John Kay he produced a roller spinning machine for cotton. In 1771 he moved to the small Derbyshire town of Cromford where he set up a large mill, driven by water wheels. In 1788 he was one of the prime movers behind a waterway to connect Cromford with the Erewash Canal at Langley Mill. The 14½ mile Cromford Canal was completed in 1794. The greatest engineering feat undertaken during its building by William Jessop and Benjamin Outram was the 3,000 yard Butterley tunnel. This tunnel had no towing path, all boats having to be legged through by the crew. It was narrow, so that wider boats coming up from the Erewash could not pass through to Cromford. Navigation could take as long as three hours, so it really was a bottle neck — and this on a canal which in 1841-2 is reputed to have carried 320,000 tons in a year. Bradshaw's of 1904 quotes:

In the tunnels of early date . . . the method of propelling boats . . . is either 'shafting' or 'legging'. . . . Legging is performed by two men, one on each side of the boat, who lie down on the forend on their backs and push against the tunnel sides with their feet. If the tunnel is too wide to admit of their reaching the side walls with their feet from the boat's deck, boards projecting over the boat's side termed 'wings' are brought into use for them to lie on.'

Thomas Frost made this rough sketch of a boat being legged through Butterley tunnel in 1845. The photograph of the east end of Butterley tunnel shows a height gauge erected to impress on crews that the tunnel had restricted headroom, the result of mining subsidence. The two spectators are sitting on the stop planks, used to seal off the tunnel should it be necessary to de-water it. It is interesting to see that a version of the height gauge appears on the 1845 sketch as well.

99

99 One of the noted engineering features of the Cromford Canal is the 200-yard-long aqueduct known as Bull Bridge over the River Amber, a road, and later the North Midland Railway. As originally built this aqueduct proved faulty and had to be extensively modified.

100

According to Farey's *General View of the Agriculture and Minerals of Derbyshire,* Volume III of 1816

over the Amber river at Bull Bridge, there is another very considerable aqueduct...built of shale freestone, consisting of a large arch for the river, and a smaller one for the mill

lead south of it, and also a gothick arch for the turnpike road, which, owing to its improper shape, is bulged a good deal, and on the north of the river is another arch for a private road under the canal.

Later E. G. Barnes in his *The Rise and Fall of the Midland Railway 1844-1874* says:

near Ambergate, the railway was to pass clean through the lofty embankment carrying the Cromford Canal. To meet statutory requirements prohibiting lengthy interference with navigation along the canal, the piers for the new aqueduct were laid very deep down and then built up to support an iron trough cast to the exact shape of the canal. Having been floated into its exact position, the trough was sunk without causing the least disturbance to the navigation.

This photograph was taken in 1945, but the aqueduct was demolished for road widening in the 1960s.

00 The promoters of the Cromford Canal had wanted it to be a through route. After its opening they planned an extension from Cromford to Bugsworth on the Peak Forest Canal, thus giving access to the north via the Peak Forest and Ashton Canals and also a new route south for the valuable limestone from the quarries around Bugsworth. Such a canal would have gone via Bakewell, but would have involved many engineering difficulties, including numerous locks. In the end the gap was bridged by a railway; the Cromford and High Peak line was opened in 1831. It was 33 miles long and was one of the most extraordinary railways in the country in that it had nine rope-worked inclines on it with conventional traction on the sections in between. The canal was included in the LMSR Act of 1944, which sanctioned abandonment. This photograph of Cromford goods wharf was taken in 1945; behind are the engine shed and repair works of the Cromford and High Peak Railway and the first of the inclines, Sheep Pasture, 1,320 yards long, rising at a gradient of one in eight and one in nine. Such inclines occasionally had a serious accident when ropes broke. A. Rimmer in his book on the Cromford and High Peak Railway says

...on 1 March 1888 when two waggons forming a descending run broke away soon after leaving the Top and ran freely down the full length of the incline. By the time they reached the bottom, they were moving very fast and failed to negotiate the curve into the goods yard at Cromford wharf. Instead, they leapt across the Cromford Canal, clearing the two tracks of the Midland Railway, which at that point are some fifteen or twenty feet below the level of the canal, and finally came to rest in a field, completely wrecked.

101 Trade on the Cromford Canal was disrupted for four years from 1889 when mining subsidence caused the partial collapse of Butterley Tunnel. In 1900 further subsidence occurred and the owners, by then the Midland Railway Company, claimed they could not afford to repair the tunnel. However, the Erewash Company, unwilling to lose the trade coming onto their canal, managed to get a Government inquiry into the problem. This inquiry drifted on; its reply did not come until 1909 when a verdict was delivered in favour of the Midland Railway. This photograph shows a busy loading scene at Cromford wharf, the head of the navigation. The picture has been inscribed by the photographer, 'Wheatcroft and Sons' wharf, August 1906'. Wheatcroft was an important carrier on the canal, even running a passenger service from Cromford to Nottingham at one time. The singe fares were 4s first class and 2s second class. The date is interesting as these pictures must have been taken after the closure of the tunnel. Thus the boats would only have been able to trade over 8¼ miles of this by now truncated system. The narrow boat *Onward* is also one of Wheatcroft's. The warehouse in the photograph was built in 1824. The horse-drawn carts seen here are typical of short haul transport for heavy loads.

102 So much of these books deal with structures or boats, that it is a pleasure to be able to include a portrait of a person who actually worked on the canal. Unfortunately, however, very little is known about this particular man, a lock keeper on the Cromford Canal. The photograph was taken in 1897 on the occasion of de Salis' visit to the Cromford. The crudity of the lock beam should be noted. It was quite common practice to use trimmed tree trunks for this purpose. The strapping post in the foreground is a particularly hefty example.

103 From Langley Mill the Cromford Canal climbs through fourteen locks in $3^1/_3$ miles. At the top of the flight is the short Pinxton branch (just over two miles long) which runs to Pinxton colliery. The locks were built to the same dimensions as those on the Erewash Canal so that wide boats could trade to the colliery wharves. A tramway from nearby Mansfield was laid to Pinxton very early in the life of the canal. This photograph is thought to date from around 1906, and shows workmen digging out Pinxton basin and removing the reeds. Presumably it had fallen into disuse, and with the closing of the tunnel it was thought that some trade might return to this branch.

103

04   The Manchester, Bolton and Bury Canal was one of a number of northern waterways built with lock sizes differing from most of the canals around it. It was originally intended to be a narrow canal, but was actually built as a wide one in the hope of joining up with the Leeds and Liverpool by extending the line from Bolton to the top of the Wigan locks. Nothing came of this Red Moss extension. Although it was a wide canal the locks were for boats only 68 feet long. Its neighbour, the Rochdale, was a standard wide canal for full length boats while the nearby Leeds and Liverpool Company built their locks above Wigan for boats only 62 feet long. This selection of craft waiting above the Nob End flight at Prestolee are known in the north of England as bastard boats. In the south they would have been just wide boats or mules. They are built on similar lines to narrow boats but to a width of 10 or 11 feet with cabins, and with a stand instead of a cratch at the fore end. For trading on the Manchester, Bolton and Bury they would have been below 68 feet in length. As on so many other family trading craft of the north the water barrel replaces the gaily painted water can. This photograph was taken in 1930 at a time when there was not a great deal of traffic on this section of the canal. It was officially abandoned in 1941 after being left waterless by the breach at Prestolee in 1936.

CANAL, NOB END, LITTLE LEVER.

105   It is surprising how much of the traffic on the Manchester, Bolton and Bury was between points on the canal itself; at one time only one sixth was coming in from other canals. This particular cargo looks like cotton from the docks at Manchester. It is obviously a light cargo as the boat is carrying so much above the hold line, even to stacking bales two deep on top of the cabin. An expecially short tiller has been fitted. The water barrel behind the chimney can still be seen. The picture is thought to have been taken around 1910 and shows a wide bastard boat climbing up three of the six staircase locks at Nob End, Prestolee. This canal ran a very successful series of passenger boats which commenced operation in october 1796. Some 60,000 or so passengers a year had been carried in this way. The journey was split at the flight of locks seen here, passengers having to get off their boat and walk down the locks to board another one at the bottom, so saving time. The service closed in 1838 with the opening of the railway from Bolton to Salford.

106 This photograph of the Manchester, Bolton and Bury Canal in 1936 shows graphically the seriousness of a breach in a canal engineered along the side of a steeply sloping valley. Because it was realised that this was a potentially weak stretch of canal, a large brick built supporting wall was constructed, and the tow path deliberately put on the valley's side to give extra strength. The breach occurred a few hundred yards from the locks seen in the previous photograph. Some of the brick reinforcement can be clearly seen in this picture along with a number of railway lines. The canal owners, the Lancashire and Yorkshire Railway, did major strengthening works during the period 1881-8. In the suspended boat on the left can be seen one of the containers which were used to carry coal. This breach was never repaired and it caused the closure of the canal as a through route.

107 At first glance it would seem strange that a canal should be built to the Westmoreland town of Kendal but proposals were made in around 1760 for a waterway to bring coal in and take away the local limestone. In 1792 John Rennie submitted plans for a 75½ mile canal from Westhoughton (between Wigan and Bolton) to Kendal. By 1796 there was traffic on a section around Preston, and the following year the line was opened through Lancaster to Tewitfield. By 1800 the Lancaster Canal had, however, failed to achieve either of its objectives. It had not reached Kendal, nor had it connected with Wigan and the waterways of the south. In 1805 the final stretch to Kendal was surveyed, but the people of that town had to wait until 18 June 1819 for the grand opening. The local council agreed to construct the actual basin in the town as well as wharves and warehouses (seen here in 1897), which were set at right angles to the line of the canal as it entered. In 1824 the canal company sold some land for Kendal gas works, thus creating a coal traffic which continued for 120 years.

108 The Lancaster Canal had a number of fine engineering structures including the Hincaster tunnel, 800 yards long, seen here. As there is no tow path boats could have been legged through it; in view of the relatively short distance, however, one suspects they were shafted through with the aid of a boat hook. There are some iron brackets on the southern entrance to the tunnel to this day, which suggests that there may have been a rope or chain hung on the side of the tunnel on which the crew could pull. While the boats were being propelled through the tunnel the horses would have been walked over the top and the horse path can be seen disappearing round the wall in the centre of the photograph. This classic scene probably dates from the late nineteenth century; by the shape in the tunnel it looks as if a trading boat is coming through to destroy the peace and quiet.

109 The Leeds and Liverpool Canal had planned a route from Blackburn to Wigan which ran almost parallel to the Lancaster Canal's truncated southern section. In 1810 the canal was complete from Leeds to Blackburn; only a short length to the west was needed to complete the full run over the Pennines. Rather than duplicate the waterways, the Leeds and Liverpool promoters came to an agreement with the Lancaster proprietors to rent their southern section from them. In return the Lancaster would build a short section from Johnson's Hillock to nearby Heapey (Wheelton) which would join up with the proposed Leeds and Liverpool from Blackburn. This short section contained the seven Johnson's Hillock locks. At the other end the Leeds and Liverpool built a connection from Wigan which included twenty-one locks. All was completed in October 1816. This photograph dates from 1895 and shows two typical Leeds and Liverpool type craft waiting at the bottom of Johnson's Hillock locks on the right. On the left is the Walton summit branch, originally connecting with the tramway to Preston. Although the tramway had ceased in the 1860s traffic on this arm continued well into the 1880s.

110 This is the eastern arm of the Lancaster Canal at Preston in 1897. The picture shows two boats typical of the type which travelled on this canal. In general they were very similar in appearance to those trading on the nearby Leeds and Liverpool Canal. Length was 72 feet and width 14 feet 6 inches. Given the right depth of water they could load 50 tons. Wooden built boats died out in the nineteenth century mainly due to the lack of adequate repair facilities — they were replaced by iron hulled boats built at Preston by W. Allsup & Sons. The hold has two beams running across it to stiffen the structure, much in the same way as narrow boats had tensioning chains to stop the sides spreading when loaded. All the boats had square sterns and a very wide deck area for the steerer who had in turn a very long tiller. The accommodation was under the covered stern area, access being obtained by steps down a companion way on the port side by the stove. This stove was normally inside the cabin and features a chimney made in two sections so that it could be easily taken down when travelling under low bridges. Usually the boat had a double bed across the stern and ventilator holes called air holes were built in either side of the stern post (as can be seen here); they were closed by slides. It was not

uncommon for other beds to be fitted in as well. Family boats were usual on this canal and this one has two window boxes of flowers on the deck. The space under the foredeck was not used for sleeping but for storage of fodder for the horse, spare lines, etc.

111 A branch of the canal was built in 1826 to the port of Glasson on the River Lune, below Lancaster. This allowed the import and export of raw materials and also made it possible for some small coasting craft to come directly onto the canals. In 1826, a sloop reached Preston from the Duddon estuary with a cargo of Cumberland slate. The following year a 60-ton sloop arrived at Kendal with salt originating from Northwich on the River Weaver. This latter journey is surprising as parts of the canal were always reputed to be shallow. Here a heavily laden boat is seen near Carnforth, about 1905; possibly because of the canal's shallowness it needs two horses to pull it. It is quite likely the boatman's son who is feeding the horses. Note the detachable towing mast placed on the tow path side of the boat. Each bridge on the Lancaster Canal had a white band painted around the arch as a safety precaution.

112　Packet boats were operated from Lancaster to Preston before 1820, for in that year the service was extended to Kendal over the newly opened top section. These boats were lightly built; covered accommodation was provided for only first class passengers. The swift or packet boats on the Lancaster Canal were limited to fifty people, taking roughly seven hours to cover 57 miles.

Trading boats were on occasions converted for the carriage of passengers. These lacked the creature comforts of the packet boat but that did not matter — such occasions were the annual outings of some local organisation. In this case it is a Zion Sunday school outing to Sedgwick near Kendal, about 1904. The boat is absolutely packed and the trip has caused so much interest that many more people have come out to watch. It would appear from the construction of the rising towpath under the bridge that this was a turn-over bridge, which allowed the tow path to change from one bank to the other in such a way that the towing horse did not have to be unhitched from its rope.

113　There were problems with finishing the south end of the Lancaster Canal as well. A section had been built from Bank Hill near Wigan to Walton, but the next 4½ miles to Preston were never completed as a waterway. Instead, the gap was crossed by a tramroad with three inclines and a bridge over the River Ribble. The railway proved much cheaper to build, due to the hilly nature of the ground to be covered. One would have thought that the transhipment of cargoes at each end would quickly make the railway uneconomic, but it lasted from 1803 until 1894. Trade on the canal gradually dwindled during the twentieth century, and in 1939 a short section of the canal in Kendal was closed. Much of the canal is still open, though it is closed between Tewitfield and Kendal. The bottom section into Preston was also closed. Here we see Preston Basin in 1897 with much railway activity, although if one looks closely a loaded boat can be seen between the two lifting bridges. The shunting of the coal wagons is being undertaken by horse traction, something which was not at all unusual on many railway sidings.

The vertical lift bridges are simple in the extreme. The presence of the securely tied rowing boat is interesting, bearing in mind that this was a busy commercial waterway.

114　This photograph is practically the same view as the previous one, but taken 63 years later (1 September 1960). This was one of a number of pictures taken by a British Railways Midland Region photographer a couple of years before the whole area was demolished, filled in and built over. It shows the squalor which can quickly set in on a waterway abandoned without adequate thought to its future. The structure projecting over the wharf allows the contents of small wagons to be tipped directly into the holds of waiting boats.

112

BITS, BRANCHES AND BASINS

Inevitably with a categorization such as has been used in this book certain stretches of waterway do not fit directly into any one section, and also there are large complexes of wharves, basins, etc, which have long been closed but are all part of the scene, and show just how vast the canal trading system must have been at one time. Bugsworth Basin (Buxworth nowadays) has always held a fascination for the author ever since a hire boat on which he was travelling broke down at the entrance on a journey to Whaley Bridge. While waiting for the mechanic the time was spent looking around at the vast number of wharves, basins and tramroads, long disused.

No excuse is given for including more pictures of Foxton, ones new to the readers, it is hoped. While most other incline planes in the country were derelict or on their last legs it really does seem strange that hardened businessmen should construct another one as late as 1900 and as elaborate as Foxton. The fact that it only lasted 12 years was due to lack of use as much as the failure of the technology involved.

115

5 The Grand Junction Canal had
veral quite long branches, most of
hich seemed to suffer from water
oubles for one reason or another.
ne of these branches was to
ickingham. As originally built, the
nal was in two parts. The first
these was the Old Stratford
anch, 1¼ miles long, which gave
e main line access to the road
affic on busy Watling Street, now
e A5. This short section was
mpleted in September 1800, with
e remaining 9½ miles to
ickingham taking only another
ght months to finish. Bridge Two
as often referred to as Old
ratford Tunnel, but was just a
ng bridge under the important
atling Street. This picture was
ken during repairs in 1926. There
as no tow path through this bridge,
the boat horses would have had to
oss the busy road above.

116 In 1840 Edward Hayes started
an agricultural engineering business
in Stony Stratford and became fairly
well known, particularly for
experiments with new forms of
machinery to help the farmer. He
also started to experiment with and
specialise in marine engines, and by
the end of the nineteenth century
was building actual boats. Among
his customers were the British
Admiralty, the Russian Government,
the French Government, and the
Egyptian Government, as well as
many port and dock authorities all
over the world. Included in his
repertoire were six tugs for the LCC
fire service and a Nile stern wheeler
as well as a Dead Sea pilgrim boat.
Most of the craft were tugs or
launches, all were built to a beam
just under the width of the Grand
Junction Canal; none had a draft of
more than four feet. Here we see
boats under construction at the yard
in 1904.

117 The firm's yard was some distance from the canal at Old Stratford, so completed hulls had to be towed along Watling Street and down Wharf Lane to the water. At first the firm used horses as the motive power, but later traction engines were employed, in this case a ploughing engine. This particular craft is a twin-screw steel-plated tug destined for the Nile. It was, incidentally, still operating there in the 1940s.

118 Once on the canal bank, the boats were set up for sideways launching, the ceremony being a highlight in village life, and watched by many people. Sometimes, it is reported, the launchings went wrong and the vessels ended up wedged across the canal. Many of the boats were fitted out afloat at Old Stratford which was satisfactory provided that the added weight did not take them over the four foot

depth of the canal. They were then towed down the Grand Junction to Brentford where the fitting out was completed, with funnels, masts, etc. Some boats went via the River Thames and the Kennet and Avon Canal to gain access to Bristol. One boat bound for Liverpool sailed from Brentford to Hull and then used the Leeds and Liverpool Canal to reach Liverpool. During the early 1900s nearly fifty men were employed in this yard. They would also tackle boats of up to ninety foot in length, but in such cases the craft would be shipped abroad in pieces, and assembled with the aid of the most modern prefabricated plans suplied by the Old Stratford yard. The firm ceased trading in 1925, hit by competition from more modern diesels and the large number of ex-WD craft coming onto the market after World War I.

119 The water supply for the Buckingham branch came from the Great Ouse, a river which it followed very closely. At Mountmill, approximately 3½ miles up the branch from Old Stratford, the canal and the river are in close company and often leakages used to occur in the canal bed and bank, which were at a higher level than the river. During the winter of 1919 the canal was closed and a 200-yard stretch given concrete walls and bed. Figures show that there were only some thirty boats a year trading over the majority of the length of the canal, say 750 tons in all, plus a little local traffic. One is surprised that these repairs were undertaken on what must have been a most uneconomical waterway. Even in 1919 it was still a case of hard work, with wheelbarrows and barrow-runs.

117

118

120 A good supply of water is essential for any canal. As artificial waterways can climb up and around obstacles by way of locks, it is necessary to locate one's primary source of water at summit level. One of the sources for the Grand Union Canal at Tring was water coming down from the Wendover Branch. Ever since it was built in 1797 this branch canal leaked, so much so that in 1897, a particularly dry year, the branch lost more water than it provided and was taking water from the summit of the Grand Junction Canal itself. This state of affairs was temporarily halted by the provision of stop planks at Little Tring, to be followed by the permanent stop lock featured here. There was little traffic over the branch by this time so the provision of only one paddle (because of only slight differences in levels) would not have hindered many boat crews. In 1901, however, a few boats did pass through to reach Buckland wharf some two miles further on from Little Tring. This photograph was taken about 1906.

The Grand Junction Canal Pumping Station, Little Tring

Photo Copyright, C. A. Howlett.

121

122

THE CANAL. WENDOVER.

121 This pair of boats belonged to Alfred Payne of Wendover and are seen here moored on the towpath side of the Wendover Branch at Buckland opposite the Gas Works. Buckland Wharf was situated through the bridge and to the left. The date of this photograph is not known. It could have been the brief period in 1901 when some boats were known to have travelled to Buckland or it could have been shortly before the stop lock was built in the late 1890s. The Paynes were an old-fashioned family of canal carriers. The cargo is not known but clearly needs side cloths to cover it.

122 The Wendover branch was planned purely as a water feeder, and to this end various mills in the Wendover area were bought by the canal company so that there could be no dispute over water rights. It was soon realised that it would not be too costly to make the feeder into a navigable channel, and an Act of Parliament to this effect was made in 1794. The canal ended some distance from Wendover itself, and a road was built out from the town to it. The wharf at Wendover was looking very derelict by the time this picture was taken in about 1910.

123 Once the dry weather was over, such water that continued to flow down the branch was directed into Wilstone reservoir, to be pumped back up to the main line. The flow along the Wendover feeder was between fourteen and forty-two locks a day. Although a trifling amount, the Grand Junction Canal Company went to great lengths and expense to keep it flowing. In 1904 the top four miles of the canal were repuddled with clay, the water level lowered and the whole used purely as a water channel taking the water direct to Wilstone reservoir. Unfortunately, this now put an extra strain onto the pumps at Tringford, which had to lift the water as much as seventy-five feet. Instead it was decided to lay a pipeline down the disused section of the canal from Drayton to the pumping station, so taking the precious water direct to the pumps.

124 This was soon found to be unsatisfactory due to the rate of variation in the flow, which played havoc with the pumps. The whole system was redesigned in 1912, the water being pumped direct into the main line, or allowed to flow into the Tringford reservoir, which was at a higher level than the one at Wilstone. This photograph, taken on May 30 1912, is believed to be the first day the new system came into operation, and it shows the intake from the water channel at Drayton.

125

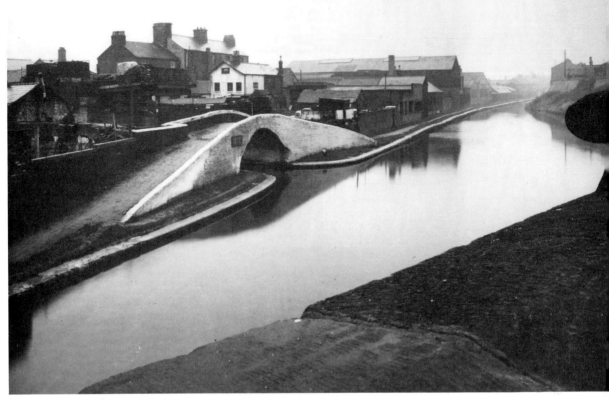

126

Stafford from the River.

5 The Newcastle-under-Lyme branch of the Trent and Mersey Canal used to leave the main line in Stoke-on-Trent. It was exactly four miles long. Most of the trade on it, according to Bradshaw, was over the first mile or so to other wharves in Stoke. It was leased to the North Staffordshire Railway, owners of the Trent and Mersey, in 1863. Nowadays, with clean air acts and active water authorities, we tend to forget that at one time parts of the canal system in this country were very badly polluted. The following account of the canal at Newcastle-under-Lyme was taken from an inquest recorded in the *Staffordshire Times* of 15 May 1875:

The water in it was inky black, and the stench intolerable. Large bubbles of gas were continually rising to the surface, being unmistakable proof of decomposing animal and vegetable matter. Three or four drains were running into it, and he saw the carcases of several dogs in various stages of decomposition floating about.

This scene of the junction of the Newcastle-under-Lyme Canal and the Trent and Mersey was taken in 1960.

126 The Staffordshire and Worcestershire Canal does not actually enter the town of Stafford. The canal was opened throughout, from the Trent and Mersey Canal at Great Haywood to Stourport on the River Severn, in 1772. As late as 1816 the canal company leased land and river access from Lord Stafford, to build a one mile navigation into Stafford itself. It left the main line near bridge 101 (Weeping Cross) and then went through Baswich (St Thomas) lock which lowered the canal to the River Sow. From here on the river was made navigable. Traffic coming in was mainly coal, and a special coal wharf was built as well as one for timber. In this picture, taken from a postcard of 1905, the River Sow is to the right, the building on the left is the Royal Brine Baths (recently demolished), and there is also a small wharf on the riverside. The tow path is in the centre of the photograph with the canal on the left. The very edge of the coal wharf can be seen. Traffic ceased on this branch some time during the 1920s although it does not seem to be very busy at the time of this picture.

127 A canal to Bradford was mooted before the Leeds and Liverpool Canal, to which it was eventually joined. In 1744 a group of 'Gentlemen, farmers and other inhabitants . . ., tried to obtain powers to make the River Aire navigable because of '. . . the heavy charges of land carriage, occasioned by the badness and unevenness of the road. . . .' The Bradford Canal, as finally built, was 3⅜ miles long, included ten locks, and was opened in 1774. The original terminus was on the edge of the town, but with added prosperity the town soon extended and the basin became much more central. As with so many canals, coal was a principal cargo, as was limestone from the Springs branch of the Leeds and Liverpool Canal at Skipton. Stone also featured as one of the principal cargoes. The closure of the canal was caused by unusual circumstances. The feeders for the canal head gradually became polluted as the urban area expanded '. . . the noxious compound is conveyed through the sluices into the canal'. An outbreak of cholera in 1849 caused the public to complain about the canal, but it was not until 1867 that it was closed and then drained. This painting by N. S. Crichton depicts the canal basin prior to its closure. It gives a good impression of the cramped nature of the then terminus.

128 The Bradford Canal was closed when it was carrying over 125,000 tons a year. Somehow the local business interest had to find alternative transport. A new company was formed and took over the drained canal, selling off the top ⅜ths of a mile, and making a new terminus lower down. Water was supplied from independent reservoirs or by pumping, so doing away with much of the pollution problem from above. The canal re-opened in 1873, but the damage to trade had been done. Many of the traders had found alternative ways of moving their products, and it was not until 1910 that the tonnage carried ever exceeded 100,000 tons in a year. The canal closed on 25th June 1922. Here in about 1900 *Victoria* of Bolton Woods (between Shipley and Bradford), owned by Butcher and Waterhouse, loads stone setts at Stonebridge. *Victoria* is a typical square sterned Leeds and Liverpool short boat built in Yorkshire with Yorkshire style square wooden chimneys in two sections, fore and aft.

129 In 1894 the Grand Junction Canal Company bought the Grand Union Canal, which extended from Norton Junction near Braunston through to Foxton and the Old Union Canal from Market Harborough to Leicester. This stretch of canal was generally in poor condition, but it was bought primarily as a water supply for the Grand Junction. The directors of the Grand Junction were persuaded by Fellows Morton and Clayton that traffic from the Nottinghamshire and Derbyshire coalfields to London could again be attracted to the canals, if this line were improved to take wide boats throughout. Rather than widen the water-consuming flight of locks at Foxton a plane was built instead. Gordon Thomas, the Grand Junction's engineer, was responsible for devising this plane and selling the idea to the canal company. The narrow boats were floated into two caissons full of water, one at the top and the other at the bottom, which were then pulled up or lowered down the plane. Gordon Thomas and his wife (centre) are seen inspecting the plane as it is under construction.

130 At the bottom of the plane two docks were built, into which the caisson descended. A guillotine gate was opened at the end of the caisson and the boats were then floated out. This photograph and the one which follows were both taken on the same day, possibly opening day, July 10 1900. The specially adapted maintenance boat belongs to the Grand Junction Canal Company, and there are crowds of people watching from the bridge in the distance. In this picture the caisson is just dropping into the bottom dock. A loaded narrow boat awaits its turn to ascend when the directors have finished their inspection. There are two boat horses and boatmen on the tow path, and the horse by the bridge appears to be wearing the traditional crotcheted ear protectors. Under the brick bridge can be seen the smaller swivel bridge erected to give tow path access to the bottom of the plane, and which still exists.

131 Earlier in the day the inspection party had taken a trip up the plane. They are seen here having just come out of the caisson into the canal proper. At the summit the caisson was pulled up in line with the top level of the canal, and a hydraulic ram then pushed it the few inches sideways to give a near watertight join. Hydraulic power was also used to raise the guillotine gates on both the docks and the caisson. It is claimed that the complete operation of the plane took twelve minutes, which would have saved nearly an hour over the use of the Foxton locks. The locks were a staircase, a flight of five, a passing pound and another set of five, and it was this lock configuration and not the number of locks which caused the hold-ups in busy periods.

132 What excitement for an outing actually to go up and down the inclined plane! This undated picture shows a pair of Northampton-based horse-drawn boats loaded with trippers on their way to the summit, the caisson having just left the wet dock at the bottom. It is surprising how leak-free the watertight guillotine gate is. Foxton inclined plane had been built in the hope that traffic over it would exceed 200,000 tons a year, but this never happened. Between 1905 and 1910 it varied between 31,417 tons and 40,767 tons. By 1908 it had been found that it was not economic to keep the engine in steam 24 hours a day, so night working was abandoned and because of this the locks were put back into good order. Gordon Thomas in his paper on the plane wrote

the capacity of the lift, allowing twelve minutes for each operation, and passing 70 tons in both directions, is 8,400 tons per twelve hours, or, approximately, 250,000 tons per annum of 300 working days. The cost of dealing with this tonnage, based on the experience of the last six weeks, inclusive of coal, oil, stores and labour, would be .05d or 1/20 of a penny per ton. The whole of the plant is operated by three men.

33 and 134 Bugsworth (later Buxworth) basin, near the head of the Peak Forest Canal at Whaley Bridge, must have been one of the largest wharf complexes on the British Canal system. On 1 May 1800 the Peak Forest Canal was opened, though a tramroad connected the top and bottom of what are now the Marple flight of locks. The quarries around Bugsworth were rich in limestone. One of the first people to use the basin was Samuel Oldnow who had lime kilns at Marple. Oldnow was one of the main promoters of the Peak Forest Canal because of his lime interests. These two commercial postcards, believed to date from around 1914, show Bugsworth when the tramways were fully occupied bringing limestone from the quarries. A guide book published in the late nineteenth century described Bugsworth as '...a thriving inland port. The basin...holds upwards of twenty longboats, it has a loading shed and stables for upward of forty large horses.' The latter remark is interesting as it seems to imply that more than twenty boats could be accommodated. Although there is only one boat visible here, some idea of the amount of traffic that this basin could carry can be gained from the lines of loaded waggons and piles of limestone. At its zenith Bugsworth village had a population of nearly 300 people; nearly all of whose employment was in some way connected with quarries, limestone or the canal.

135 This photograph shows part of the complex of wharves and warehouses at Bugsworth around 1930 after trade from the quarries had ceased and the scrap men had removed the hundreds of tramroad waggons which had littered the sidings. The building on the right is a warehouse into which ran another arm of the canal. The tramway lines are clearly seen behind, leading up the valley. By the far building on the right (a tramway workshop) a branch turned sharp right to tunnel through to Barren Clough Quarry. The main line of the tramway continued up the valley to Dove Hole Quarries 6½ miles away. In the centre of the picture are lines of the tramway which can be seen ending in a raised section by the wharf. The structure at the end of this is a waggon tippler for unloading direct into waiting boats. On the left can be seen the bottom of the lime kilns which were normally discharged straight into the boats. Behind centre the bread van is delivering to one of the two pubs on the site. The wharves have been derelict since this picture was taken, though the basin is now being painstakingly, if slowly, restored by the Inland Waterways Protection Society.

136

137

The tramways leading to ...gsworth Basin were interesting. ...hey were of the usual Outram ...ateway type to a gauge of 4 feet 2 ...ches. Working in this area of the ...ak District must have been ...duous. The plateway was some 6½ ...les long and included an 85 yard ...nnel, and a 209 feet inclined ...ane. The tramroad rose to a height ...1,139 feet. The canal company ...ntrolled the plateway as well as ...e quarries, and from all accounts ...ems to have been a good employer, ...en down to providing a store ...hich sold their workers goods at ...st price. This photograph was ...ken around 1905 and shows a ...pical horsedrawn tramroad truck ...the Peak Forest system, although in ...is case a human cargo takes the ...ace of limestone.

...7   On 21 March 1776 the ...idgewater Canal was opened ...rough to the hamlet of Runcorn, ...e point which the Duke of ...idgewater had chosen as his ...rminus and where he built a flight ...locks taking his canal down to the ...ver Mersey. The coming of the ...nal to Runcorn had the effect of doubling the population in the years between 1801 and 1821. The traffic on the Runcorn flight of locks was so great that a second set of locks was built in 1827. With the coming of the Manchester Ship Canal, the Bridgewater Navigation Company, owners of the Mersey and Irwell, sold out to the Ship Canal Company. The route of the Mersey and Irwell was required for the ship canal. With the completion of the Ship Canal in 1894 the locks were cut off from the River Mersey, but this made little difference to the traffic. Over more recent years the pattern of trade changed and in 1939 the original locks (the old road) were closed. By 1963, the date of this photograph, the new road was practically derelict. In this picture, taken from Waterloo Bridge, the remains of the old road can be seen on the right. The River Mersey is in the background and the Manchester Ship Canal can just be seen at the bottom of the flight of locks.

138   Narrow boats used to congregate in the dock at the foot of the flight of locks. It was a favourite place to find boats from the Anderton Company, as we see here. This scene is typical, with two families talking while awaiting another cargo. This firm started as Alexander Reid and Company and changed to Anderton Company in 1836, a name which it retained even after merging with the Mersey, Weaver and Ship Canal Carrying Company as late as 1954. The fleet was sold to British Waterways in 1958. The reason for the success of this company at a time when so many other carrying concerns went to the wall was that they kept to a regular series of routes, using customers who mostly had canalside factories and works. The Anderton Company specialised in cargoes for the potteries, bringing up from the docks many different bulky cargoes such as china clay and stone. The cargoes down to the docks from the Five Towns would normally be crates of earthenware and crockery. The boat's name, carved into the counter, was a feature of the Anderton boats as were their rounded sides, rounded because when loaded with light top-heavy crates, they would roll easily, but always come upright.

138

139 We are lucky to have a record of what is possibly the last ever journey up the flight of locks at Runcorn, which was accomplished by John Seymour in a British Waterways pleasure boat some two years after the Bridgewater Company thought that they were impassable! Here is an extract from his excellent book *Voyage into England.*

The locks looked not only dry, but wrecked. They were rubbish filled, and many of the gates were perished and broken. The short pounds between them had been partially filled in with sunken Bridgewater barges and these, mudfilled, had started to fall to pieces... and the whole scene was desolate and sad, yet the locks had been perfect when I had gone up the flight in *Jenny the Third* only seven years earlier...at that time there had been a fleet of narrow boats, loaded with coal, waiting there [at the top] and we had made friends with an old lady and a young girl who worked on one of them. Now there were no working boats...

The locks were in good working order when De Salis climbed them in *Dragon Fly*, seen here in June 1895.

Before readers pick up their
ns and write to the publisher, the
thor readily acknowledges that he
stretching his rules by including
s picture. The *Warrington
ardian* for Saturday 11 July 1874
d an item as follows:

e Bridgewater Canal Navigation
mpany have this week
augurated what will no doubt
ove to be a useful and profitable
provement. They have placed on
canal a screw tug steamer to be
lowed speedily by others for the
rpose of dragging their barges,
us superseding horse power.

entually some twenty-six of these
ry distinctive canal tugs were in
vice. Their home was the area
ound the top lock at Runcorn and

Waterloo Bridge. In fact they used a
dry dock under the arch of the
bridge on which the photographer is
standing, and it is this dry dock and
the section of the canal beyond
which no longer exists today. This
photograph shows at least thirteen of
these tugs preparing for a day's work
in around 1910. The tugs never
worked down the Runcorn flight
with a tow, as no craft were allowed
down under power (they had to be
bow-hauled). They did tow boats on
the Manchester Ship Canal, also on
the Mersey and Irwell Navigation. It
can be seen that the tugs have wheel
steering at the stern. Access to the
smoke box (for sweeping the tubes) is
through the hatch in front of the
funnel (open on left hand boat).

141 Apsley South End Wharf at
the Dickinson paper mill in
Hertfordshire must have been
typical of so many factory wharves
up and down the country in the days
of commercial traffic. John
Dickinson's fleet of boats was owned
by Fellows Morton and Clayton and
worked a regular run from Apsley,
Nash, Home Park and Croxley Mills
down the Grand Union to
Dickinson's Paddington depot. Their
principal cargoes were finished paper
products down to Paddington, and
rags and similar waste products up
to the mills for pulping. The
boatmen on this run were often
known as 'the paper dashers'. The
circular chimneys suspended from
the roof are a relic from the days
when steam-powered narrow boats
operated from the wharf. The
steamers used to lie with their
funnels immediately under one of
these chimneys. With the cessation
of commercial traffic to this wharf in
the 1950s it fell into disuse.

INTRODUCTION

Introduction to Part 2

In the introduction to volume one of this book I tried to trace briefly the history of our canal system, so that the reader could readily understand why so many canals had fallen into disuse. I outlined the way in which coal was moved underground in the Duke of Bridgewater's mines at Worsley near Manchester in the 1760s, and told how it was the same Duke with John Gilbert and James Brindley who built Britain's first canal from these mines to the city of Manchester. Because of the very poor state of the roads at that time, water transport was more reliable and much cheaper. When the Bridgewater Canal opened in 1761, it is said that the price of coal in Manchester fell from 7d to 4d a cwt. After this there occurred a phenomenon now known as 'canal mania', in which nearly every town or village in the country seemed to want a canal. Many were planned; some were built but others only half finished. The canals held sway as the major transport system of goods, and some passengers, until the 1850s when the railways started to make their presence felt. The railway era had commenced with the Liverpool and Manchester Railway in 1830. Because all the canals were owned by private companies, as were the railways, there was little co-operation between the two types of transport. Certainly little attempt was made to integrate them. For one reason or another the railways took over a number of canals beween 1845 and 1847, and in that time 948 miles of canal came under railway control. The railways wanted the canals for a number of reasons; either to build on, as the canals had in many cases taken the most advantageous and the flattest routes; or to stifle them because of their competition. A number of canal companies were pleased to sell up, as their canals were not particularly profitable, and they could see the railways being very stiff opposition.

Amazingly enough, the canals, in their best years, were far more prosperous than the railways ever were. Another disadvantage with the canals being privately owned was that, in many cases, neighbouring canals were constructed to a different gauge. Boat owners also had to deal separately with each company, so that it was very difficult to negotiate special terms, particularly for long-haul transport. Even so, it was still possible for the canals to be competitive. The following figures

came from a small notebook kept by the clerk to the Wolver[c] Paper Mill at Oxford, which in 1884 was using around 100 t[o] of coal a week, all of which which was brought in by water. [T] coal was Moira licence slack coming down the Ash[by] Coventry and Oxford Canals, a journey of some 100 miles. [T] cost per ton in 1884 was 13s 4d. The clerk has also worked [out] the pro rata cost by rail for the same trip, including carriage [by] road from the sidings in Oxford to the Mill, and this was 13s [?] per ton. The same figures for 1916 are 19s 8¾d by canal and [?] 11d by rail. I strongly suspect that if it had been possible for [the] mill to have a siding laid direct from the railway, then rail tra[ffic] would have been a cheaper proposition. This type of ca[nal] traffic, coal from colliery side to factory side, was the very [last?] traffic on the canal system in 1970. Incidentally, Wolverc[ote?] Mill continued taking coal by water right up until the 7 M[ay?] 1952, when modernisation and re-building took place an[d a] change was made to oil firing, which in turn was augmented [by] North Sea gas.

The canals in this book are of three distinctly different typ[es.] Those canals which ran 'down to the sea', and which often h[ad] no other connection with the rest of the canal system, and h[ad] no through traffic, so they were entirely dependent on th[eir] own resources. Many of them were closed before photograp[hy] became popular, and the author has had considera[ble] difficulty in finding pictures of many of these canals when th[ey] were open to traffic. The canals of the South Wales Valleys [all] ran down from the heads of the valleys to the docks, carryi[ng] the products or the demands of the industrial revolutic[n.] These canals were safe until the railways came into the valle[ys] and connected up the collieries and the works to the main li[ne,] thus opening up trade all over the country without the need [for] transhipment at the docks. There was no connecti[on] whatsoever between the canals of South Wales and the ca[nal] system in the rest of the country. 'From East to West' [in] particular, deals with the Kennet and Avon, a canal which in [its] later years suffered from severe neglect at the hands of [its] railway owners. Happily, it is also one of the canals which ha[s a] very active preservation society working on it, and, in t[he] forseeable future, it will re-open over its full length.

e greatest canal crossing in Britain is undoubtedly the Leeds
1 Liverpool, still happily with us, never having closed, and
refore out of the scope of this book. Two others which might
ve come into this section were the Rochdale Canal and the
ddersfield Narrow Canal, but as they both lead into the
lder and Hebble, which is still open, they have been covered
ewhere.

This leaves us with the major crossings of the country in the
th: the Kennet and Avon, the Wilts and Berks, the North
lts, the Thames and Severn and the Stroudwater
vigation. It was James Brindley who first linked the two
in navigations in the north, the river Trent and the river
rsey, and then joined them with the river Thames and
vern with a meeting of them all somewhere in the middle.
wever, London to the Bristol Channel or the Severn estuary

Birmingham was not a very good through route. The
portance of Bristol as a port at these times must not be
derestimated, but what all these canal promoters wanted
s access for trade to and from the South Wales ports. Coal
m the Forest of Dean was also important and for that reason
mall reference has been made to the wharves at Bullo Pill, a
st important loading point for cargoes for the Stroudwater
nal and beyond. Somerset miners actively opposed any
empts to bring in South Wales and Forest of Dean coal, by
but destroying Saltford Lock on the River Avon in 1738.
The Great Western Railway, owners of the Kennet and
on Canal, ran the canal for many years at a considerable loss.
win Pratt writing in 1906 says:

Altogether it costs the Great Western Railway Company

about £1 to earn each 10s. they receive from the Canal; and
whether or not, considering present day conditions of trade
and transport, and the changes that have taken place
therein, they would get their money back if they spent still
more on the canal, is, to say the least of it, extremely
problematical. One fact absolutely certain is that the canal
is already capable of carrying a much greater amount of
traffic than is actually forthcoming, and that the absence of
such traffic is not due to any neglect of the waterway by its
present owners. Indeed, I had the positive assurance of
Mr. Saunders that, in his capacity as Canals Engineer to
the Great Western, he had never yet been refused by his
Company any expenditure he had recommended as
necessary for the efficient maintenance of the canals under
his charge. . . . I believe that any money required to be
spent for this purpose would be readily granted. I already
have power to do anything I consider advisable to keep the
canals in proper order.

This is of course the Great Western party line. Evidence given
to the Royal Commission on Canals and inland waterways
showed that the Kennett and Avon tolls were 50 per cent
higher than those on comparable waterways.

It must also be concluded that promoters of east-to-west
waterways always looked to through traffic for their mainstay.
This did not always materialise in the quantities expected,
trade tending to flow up or down from the centre. It is also
doubtful if there would ever have been enough water in the
summit pounds of many of these canals, even in the lower lying
south, to sustain the through traffic originally expected.

1 'Of the good effects arising from a
well regulated system of inland
navigation there can be no doubt; but at
the same time it should be recollected
that in most instances these effects
must be produced by slow and gradual
means. There is probably no canal in
Great Britain to which this observation
may be applied with greater propriety
than the Kennet and Avon. The
difficulties to be encountered have
sometimes been so great, as to present a
very unpromising appearance as to its
ultimate execution. . . .' With these
words, Priestley sums up some of the
problems of the Kennet and Avon
Canal Navigation, which joined the
Thames at Reading with the Avon at
Hanham Lock eleven miles below Bath.
Strictly the canal is from Newbury to
Bath, the Kennet navigation links
Newbury with the River Thames and
the River Avon navigation Bath with
Bristol. Built as a wide waterway it not
only enjoyed much through traffic but

Kennet and Avon Canal.

In Pursuance of an Act of Parliament passed in the 34th
Year of the Reign of his Majesty King George the Third,
intituled

"An Act for making a Navigable Canal from the River
"KENNET, at or near the Town of Newbury, in the
"County of Berks, to the River AVON, at or near
"the City of Bath, and also certain Navigable Cuts
"therein described"

This Ticket certifies that *Francis Smith*
is a Proprietor of this Undertaking and intitled to
a Share therein numbered *2741*

In Testimony whereof the Common
Seal of the Company is hereunto affixed
this Eighteenth Day of April, in the Year
of our Lord One Thousand Seven Hundred
and Ninety-four.

generated a lot from wharves along its
length. This shows an early share
certificate of 1794.

Water supply was a problem on the summit level near Savernake in Wiltshire. As originally planned the summit was to have been 15 miles long, but this would have included a 2½-mile tunnel. To avoid this heavy engineering, the route was changed and the summit shortened to 2 miles only, hence the water problems. Suitable supplies could not be found at the summit level so water had to be pumped up from a reservoir known as Wilton Water some 40ft below it. The first steam engine began pumping here in November 1809. It was a Boulton and Watt engine which had originally been built for the West India Dock Company but not used. It was replaced in 1846 by a new Cornish beam engine. John Rennie ordered another engine which commenced pumping in 1812. These engines are still in situ in the engine house at Crofton and the 1812 (modified to the Cornish cycle in 1843) continued to pump until 1958. A diesel pump was then installed followed by a more permanent electric one. Both engines have now been restored by the Crofton Society and are some of the earliest beam engines working on steam anywhere in the world. This picture shows the beams of the two engines, photographed when they were in daily use around 1910. The beam in the fore-ground is that of the 1845 engine. These massive beams rest in large bearings, which are in turn supported on the beam wall which carries the working load of the engine down into the foundations of the building.

4

The steam chests and cylinder heads of both engines with that of the 1845 engine in the foreground. The photograph again being taken in 1910.

The 1812 engine a year or so before it came out of regular service in 1959. This is a first-class view of cylinder head and valve gear, also part of the parallel motion. The main reason for cessation of steam pumping was the fact that the top twenty or so feet of the chimney outside the building had to be removed because it was dangerous and as a result insufficient draught was available to keep the boiler fires burning correctly. Since preservation a fan has been installed to compensate for this missing draught.

5

6

One of the major engineering features of the Kennet and Avon Canal is the magnificent aqueduct designed by John Rennie over the River Avon near Limpley Stoke. Constructed in the Doric style it has three spans and an overall length of 150ft. Over the centre arch two tablets have been erected, the inscription on the north side being 'To the memory of John Thomas by whose skill, perseverence and integrity the Kennet and Avon Canal was brought to prosperous completion AD MDCCCX [1810]. The proprietors gratefully inscribed this tablet AD MDCCCXXVIII [1828].' John Thomas was the superintendent of works under Rennie from 1802. The south side reads 'To Charles Dundas, chairman of the Kennet and Avon Canal Company from its inception. The proprietors, mindful of his important services and his unremitted exertions through a period of XL [40] years gratefully erected this tablet AD MDCCCXXVIII [1828].' Dundas was the chairman of the second meeting on 6 April 1788 which proposed the building of the canal and he remained connected with it for the next forty-four years, until his death in 1832, and because of his connection, the aqueduct was named after him. The date of this photograph is June 1953. On the left of Dundas wharf can be seen the remains of the junction with the Somersetshire Coal Canal. The first lock was by the house next to the basin. The wharf crane and warehouse can just be seen on the wharf.

6   During the latter part of the nineteenth century there were many complaints from traders on the canal that the water levels were low and that it was not possible for them to load their boats fully due to the risk of grounding. Whilst the published depth of the canal was 5ft it was often much less than this in reality. A regulating factor however was the sill on the Dundas Aqueduct which when full only allowed boats drawing 4ft 1in to pass over without grounding. This is a view looking down on to Dundas Wharf by the end of the acqueduct and was taken on 14 December 1926. The Somersetshire Coal Canal joined the Kennet and Avon on the right of this picture.

7   Another aqueduct on the Kennet and Avon Canal which is impressive but always over-shadowed by Dundas is the one at Avoncliffe. The main span is of 60ft with two subsidiary flood arches as at Dundas. This photograph was taken in 1910 when the aqueduct was closed for repairs and had been emptied of water. As at Dundas the railway also shares the same valley, and when it was being built it had to pierce the canal embankment by an extra arch. While it was being built the canal company requested compensation should they have to close the waterway for any length of time. £500 was asked for the first week, plus £100 per day after that. This kept the railway engineers on their toes, and only £800 was paid in all. Samuel Smiles is reputed to have said of John Rennie's architecture 'Wherever there is an acqueduct or a bridge upon the line of this canal, it will be found excellent in workmanship and tasteful in design.'

7

When the Kennet and Avon Canal
s built, one obstacle held up the final
ening for some years. This was the
at flight of locks at Caen Hill,
vizes. There are twenty-nine locks in
flight but fifteen of them arise one
er the other in a long, straight line
d in their heyday must have indeed
en 'one of the wonders of the
terways'. The flight of wide locks
vers 2 miles and lifts the canal 237ft.
order that these locks should not be
wasteful of water, the pounds
tween fifteen of the locks were
ended sideways to provide extra
kage water. This was an idea of
nnie's and undertaken at the time of
ginal construction. In 1803 the canal
ched the bottom of the works and
orsedrawn tramway was laid to
nnect the two ends of the canal until
locks were finished. In this post
orld War II photograph the
ension pounds have started to silt
. The town of Devizes can be seen at
top of the flight. Note that the road
dge at the bottom has no tow path
ough it beside the canal; a separate
dge is provided. This must have
en very inconvenient when working
rse-drawn boats due to having to
hitch the towing line.

9 Very few photographs seem to exist
which show boats actually using the
Caen Hill flight of locks. This scene is
thought to be around 1880, and shows a
pair of narrow boats at the bottom of
the straight stretch of these locks.
These traders are lucky — all the locks
seem to be set for them! The boat on
the right is well decorated while the
left-hand one has not been so well cared
for. The traditional can of drinking
water has been replaced by a barrel.
Only a few years after the canal was
built traffic was so heavy that working
through these locks at night was
commonplace, and gas lighting was
installed. The company minute book
records, on 26 October 1829, 'the gas
works along the line of locks at Devizes
being now in operation — resolved that
no barge or boat be allowed to enter any
one of the Devizes locks after the gas
shall be lighted but on payment of one
shilling for each barge and 6d. for each
boat, which payment shall entitle the
owner to navigate his barge or boat
through the said locks so long as the gas
shall be lighted, but no longer.'

10

11

12

The Carr-Ellisons, besides velling over the canal system in their nverted narrow boat *Susan Sheila* e Montgomeryshire Canal, in lume 1, Plate 71), had previously ned and travelled in a narrow beam am launch *Thetis*. In October 1931 ey took *Thetis* over the length of the nnet and Avon Canal, and as the terway was not well maintained at t time, Carr-Ellison managed to rsuade the manager to loan him mbers of the canal staff employed by e Great Western Railway to help m through the locks. 'One of the gthmen who joined us today, by me Old Tom, was a most amusing aracter and a great tea drinker, and ough having lost half his tongue m an operation for cancer he became te incoherent in his speech after oking a cigarette. . . . During the rse of the morning our propeller ame badly fouled with a length of and wire to which a horseshoe had come attached in some mysterious y, and this necessitated Joe stripping cold blood whilst the ladies turned ir backs and going over the side, ich he did most manfully, though weather and the water were tinctly "parky".' (Extract from rr-Ellison's personal diary/log.) etis is seen here descending the locks Caen Hill, Devizes.

11 A number of different types of craft were tried, in early years, to find the most satisfactory way of carrying passengers and light freight. The boat seen here is a swift boat of light construction developed on the Scottish canals. Quite a few swift boats were introduced on the English waterways — eg Lancaster (see Volume 1, Plate 112). The iron boat *The Swallow* was purchased by the Kennet and Avon Canal Company in 1833 for £150. The route chosen was Bath to Bradford-on-Avon. By 1837 there were two trips daily and accommodation was provided in first and second class cabins. The boat is seen approaching the fourteenth-century tithe barn at Bradford-on-Avon. It is interesting to note that after the canal had been taken over by the Great Western Railway, this 'Scotch' boat continued to run on a once-a-day basis in the summer only, but then it was not allowed to carry parcels. The railway also restricted its speed to 4mph.

12 One of the principle traders based on the Kennet and Avon was the firm of Robbins and Company, of Honey Street. They brought a lot of timber up the canal from places between Avonmouth and Hungerford to their yards at Honey Street, near Pewsey. This photograph, taken about 1904, is of Honey Street itself and some of the large tree boles can be seen on the left-hand side of the picture. On the right is the slip of their boat building business which prospered for many years. They built wide craft known as Kennet barges, which were also used on the River Wey, the Basingstoke Canal and the River Avon. They also built trows. Boats would be built under the covered dock and launched sideways into the canal. The narrowboat seen here is typical of one working on river navigations and tideways, because of its high bulwarks at the fore end. The small boat in the background on the left-hand bank is the one provided by the canal company for ferrying people across the waterway. A right-of-way had been cut, and no bridge had been provided.

13 Robbins and Company were known, from about 1900, as Robbins, Lane and Pinniger Limited. By the 1930s they had sold the majority of their fleet of boats, only retaining the Kennet style barge *Unity,* which had been built at their Honey Street yard in 1896. *Unity* was capable of carrying 60 tons of cargo given a good depth of water, and is seen here about to enter Bruce Tunnel at Savernake. The crew is preparing to propel the boat through the 502-yard tunnel. Bradshaw says that the boats were hauled through by means of a chain fixed to the side walls; although these are not in evidence in this picture, they are still in existence on the southernmost wall. The photograph is thought to have been taken around 1910. *Unity* was last used in 1933, and although timber was still being taken to Honey Street as late as 1937, by then the boats were on hire from the traders Francis and Niblett. Robbins, Lane and Pinniger ceased trading in 1950.

14 This charming wharfside scene could have been taken at any small country wharf between, say, 1800 and 1900. The cargo is possibly wheat; it is being loaded by a typical hand-powered wharf crane direct from the miller's or farmer's cart into the boat. Narrowboat *Croxley* comes from the fleet run from this wharf at Devizes by William Dickenson. He was a general trader between Devizes, Bristol and Avonmouth. Kenneth Clew in his book on the Kennet and Avon Canal recalls that local traders found Dickensons so reliable that they consigned their goods by canal long after most people were sending them by rail. The firm stopped trading in the mid 1920s due mainly to competition from road transport.

15 Pleasure boating is a recent phenomenon. There was a boat hire firm on the Shropshire Union Canal near Chester in 1935, but this was unusual. A number of canals had boat stations at which skiffs or canoes could be hired by the hour. Some of the prettier waterways with little commercial traffic had trip boats, and the one operating from Llangollen is perhaps the best known. This photograph, copied from a postcard, is thought to have been taken in the 1920s, and shows such a trip boat. On the back of the postcard is the following message 'the other day we went to Bradford-on-Avon in this boat on the canal. It was lovely, we went over the aqueduct.' Though the card is not postmarked, no doubt the lady boarded the boat in Bath, most probably at Darlington Wharf, for the ten-mile-trip to Bradford-on-Avon, travelling over both the Avoncliffe and Dundas aqueducts.

13

THE CANAL. BATHAMPTON.

16/17 This photograph is of a total stoppage on the canal at Hungerford around 1910, when it was necessary to renew a culvert which went under the waterway. The canal would have been blocked off by the nearest stop planks either side of the place to be worked on, for the wattle dam on the right would only be protection from a small flow of water, leaking through past the stop planks. The area being worked on under the bed of the canal is being drained by means of an Archimedes screw, a somewhat crude device which requires continual turning of the handle to transfer water up the screw and out by the feet of the winder. The wet mud on the left shows it to have been used recently. This particular screw was in existence until relatively recently at Devizes, and the other photograph of it shows it on the wharfside there in October 1932. Three other Archimedes screws were recently found sunk in the canal at Hungerford. The sheerlegs on the left have been erected to lower something heavy down into the hole, possibly pipes for the culvert.

18/19 Relatively little has been written about air raid damage to Britain's canals in World War II The Kennet and Avon Canal received at least two direct hits in the Bath area on the nights of 26 and 27 April 1942. The first photograph shows part of the damage to one of the Widcombe flight of locks, photographed ten days later. As the canal was not being used to help the war effort, little attempt was made to repair the damage quickly. The second photograph shows damage to Locksbrook Bridge sustained in the same raid. In 1948 the Railway Executive tried to persuade the British Transport Commission to close the canal, but without success. The waterway lingered on, with a number of brave attempts made to navigate or even trade over part of it. In July 1951 Caen Hill locks were declared unsafe and padlocked shut. The canal was never abandoned, however; slowly

public opinion won the day, influenced by the Kennet and Avon Canal Trust, and at last restoration is now in hand. The crucial event which saved the day was Parliamentary refusal to allow the British Transport Commission (No 2) Bill to close the canal in 1956.

20 Though the canal was almost impassable by the late 1940s the Earl of Lucan's 70ft narrow boat *Hesperus* took in the complete length of the waterway in 1948 on a trip which started at Broxbourne in Hertfordshire and ended in Manchester. One of the crew members, George Day, was an experienced Kennet and Avon boatman and made a unique log of this trip in rhyme. From Reading to Newbury they took in tow a landing craft named *Faith Hope and Charity*.

By nightfall only inches make
Although our arms and hands they ache.
Owner here he slipped off bank,
Crawled out of water looking damp.
Through locks we haul out clear of weeds
To find pounds choked for miles
     with reeds.
We crush these down beneath our keel,
Canal gang here so tired they reel. . . .

. . . Stanton St Bernard soon was passed,
The weed and mud soon held us fast,
For thirteen hours on tackle heaved
Twas nine pm before we're freed. . . .

. . . From Horton Bridge we're took in tow
By eighteen men. The going's slow.

This photograph shows *Hesperus* arriving at Newbury with *Faith, Hope and Charity* in tow.

21 While coal has been mined in Somerset since the fifteenth century, the problem has always been one of transporting it to the industrial areas that will use it in quantity. With the coming of the Kennet and Avon Canal, linking the Thames with the Bristol Channel, it was thought that the collieries at Radstock and High Littleton could now have water transport. The Somerset Coal Canal was authorised by Act of Parliament in 1794. The proposed branch to Radstock, though completed as a canal, was never linked to the main line at Midford and in 1815 it was converted into a tramroad. The Somersetshire Coal Canal's seal is one of the most attractive and explicit of all such heraldry. At the top left is a rendering of Old Father Thames showing that they expected trade to be carried on right through the Kennet and Avon Canal system to the River Thames, and London. Top right is a very well-engraved beam engine with delightful

external haystack boiler. This is a colliery pumping engine, commemorating the association with the coal mines. Bottom left is a Severn trow symbolising the expected trade from the Severn Estuary and Bristol Channel. The sword, waves and fortified walling are the arms of the City of Bath, one of the nearer urban areas which would benefit from cheaper coal.

22 One of the problems on the Somersetshire Coal Canal was the hill at Combe Hay. First the promoters experimented with the caisson lock, where a boat was to have been floated into a watertight box and lowered 46ft in a massive shaft to the lower canal level. The crews remained in the caissons — which must have been an extremely claustrophobic experience. This lock was completed in 1798 and trials did begin; the promoters had, however, turned to the idea of an inclined plane. This was opened in 1801, but was extremely inconvenient in use. Also, the transhipment from boat to truck and back to boat broke up the lumps of coal; moreover, double handling was very slow and expensive. After raising extra capital from both the Kennet and Avon and Wilts and Berks Canals, conventional locks were built. Combe Hay flight was one of the toughest obstacles of any waterway — twenty-two locks in just over a mile. Even though there had been brisk trade in its earlier years — Bath benefitted, for example, by a reduction of a third in the cost of coal — railway competition and the high costs of maintenance and pumping water up the locks caused the

canal to go into liquidation in 1893. This photograph was taken early in the 1950s and shows part of the Combe Hay flight of locks, 50 or so years after closure.

23/24 'I looked and, under the bridge, drawing after him a light punt-shaped boat, came an old man with white hair and a soft hat that partially concealed it. "Who is he" I asked. "Keeps the hedges along the canal in order. Trims them up a bit so that the horses can pass by." "But no barges come along here, surely," said I. "We haven't seen one all the way from Sapperton." "Don't say that to him, sur. He goes on working here day after day all year round, and every night he goes home he expects to find a letter from the canal company telling him he ain't wanted no longer. Don't tell him we haven't seen no barges, sur"....' (E. Temple Thurston *The Flower of Gloster*, first published in 1911.) Temple Thurston was recalling a conversation with his boatman, Eynsham Harry, as they met up with Willum, the lengthsman, on the Thames and Severn Canal, who was responsible for maintenance on the stretch from Lechdale to Latton. In June 1783 the first work started in the task of joining the River Thames with the River Severn. In November 1789 the first boat sailed onto the Thames, having come along the completed canal route. Tremendous problems followed some of which will be apparent from the following pictures. Temple Thurston must have been one of the last people to navigate right through.

21

22

25 One of the problems which the owners of the Thames and Severn canal never overcame was that of water supply. A wind pump was installed near Thames Head on the summit pound right from the start of through traffic, but it was soon seen to be inadequate. A Boulton and Watt steam engine replaced it in 1793; this continued pumping until it received a general overhaul in 1833. Twenty years later it was worn out. Humphrey Household in his definitive book on the Thames and Severn takes up the story: 'In October 1853, the committee authorised him to go ahead, and in little over six months, Taunton had found, bought, and installed a second-hand engine built in 1852 by Thomas and Company of the Charlestown Foundry for Wheal Tremar, near Liskeard, and scarcely used before the mine closed down. . . . the parts were shipped from Looe, . . . on 8 February 1850, the day after the vessel had arrived in the Severn, dismantling of the Boulton and Watt engine began, and as the new engine was set to work on 28 April, the pump was out of action for little more than 11 weeks.' The main problem, however, was that the bed of the canal was porous and the water simply seeped through, hence by the late 1800s the canal was impassable in places. This photograph is of the Thomas engine taken in 1895, with the canal looking derelict.

26 The greatest engineering feat on the Thames and Severn Canal was Sapperton Tunnel, 3,817yd long, which took 5 years to complete. While workmen battled on to finish the tunnel this small settlement called Daneway became the terminus for the canal on the Stroud side. The locks shown here are the twenty-seventh and twenty-eighth in the climb up the Golden Valley. Here the canal widened out with a wharf on the right-hand side and a small enclosed basin running out of the picture on the right. The cottage is that of the wharfinger, while the building on the left is the Daneway Inn. The photograph is thought to have been taken around 1904. The water level in the pound looks to be 2-3ft below normal.

27 The by-laws specifically forbade boats to be propelled through Sapperton tunnel by means of 'shafts sticks or other things . . .' so Temple Thurston travelled through Sapperton tunnel the hard way. 'Sometime ago, when there was more constant traffic this canal, there were professional leggers to carry you through; for there is no tow path, and the barge must be propelled by the feet upon the side walls of the tunnel. Now that the barge pass so seldom this profession has become obsolete. There are no legger now. For four hours Eynsham Harry and I lay upon our sides on the wings that are fitted to the boat for that purpose, and legged every inch of the 2¾ miles. It is no gentle job. Countless were the times I have looked ahead to that faint pin-point of light; for by such infinite degrees did it grow larger as we neared the end, that I thought we should never reach it. "What used the leggers to be paid?" I asked . . . "5s. Sir, for a loaded boat. 2s. 6d. for an empty one."' Unfortunately, Temple Thurston did not photograph his boat the tunnel, but one of the last boats to go through must have been this outing of pupils from the Brimscombe Polytechnic who are reputed to have gone through the tunnel and back in 1912. (A note on the original photograph added later says 'more like 1910'). It would seem that the folk here had used 'shafts or sticks or other things' to propel them through. This the west, or Daneway, end.

28 In February 1955 Philip Weaver accompanied by his son Rodney, and Bob Penney, made a survey of the tunnel as it was then. This photograph was taken at or near the 20-chain plate looking towards the south-east portal (Coates end). This is the end of the tunnel, which, when being built, had be completely lined with brick as it was the section bored through Greater Oolite.

29 Inside the tunnel at the 51-chain mark from the south-east portal and looking towards it. This point is almost under the railway cutting where the railway crosses over the canal tunnel. The rough, unnatural hewn state of the walls can be clearly seen. The pin-point in the distance is the tunnel entrance.

30 This photograph was taken at or near the 82-chain mark in from the south-east portal but is looking toward the Daneway end. This is the point of major roof collapse. Bob Penney is examining one of the oak reinforcing timbers put in to strengthen the invert of the tunnel when it was repaired in 1916. Over the years these have decayed and have been forced upward and fractured by pressures exerted from the walls.

31 The Great Western Railway controlled the canal for a little while and tried to close it, but without success. Later they passed it on to a trust made up of the representatives of the local authority and local canal companies, as well as the railway. The trust spent £19,000 on making the canal navigable once again and the waterway opened to traffic in 1895. By 1901 it was closed again due to leakage of water in various places. Gloucestershire County Council then took over and spent £30,000 in the next ten years. Much of this money was spent concreting the bottom at the worst parts where leakage was most prevalent. In this photograph Gloucestershire County Council workmen are repairing Puck Mill lower lock in 1907. This picture very clearly shows the way in which the top gates of the lock seal against the stout wooden arrow-shaped elm baulks of the lock sill.

32 The Gloucestershire County Council had not originally intended to spend a lot of money on Puck Mill lower lock, nor the pound above it, but apparently it leaked so badly that it emptied itself overnight every night. Here concrete is being used to repair the bed of the canal and much of it is being brought in on the contractor's narrow-gauge railway laid along both sides of the waterway. What looks like a workman's punt with a cabin is moored across the bottom of the lock.

33 Gloucestershire County Council struggled on trying to keep the canal open, but stoppages of up to twelve weeks became necessary in 1905, 1906, 1907 and 1908. The exact date of this photograph of the locks leading up to Sapperton is not known, but is thought to be prior to 1910. The works appear to be in good order but the bed is dry. The ground paddle gear is seen clearly, but it is unusual for it to be facing up the canal. It is more normally mounted in the wing walls of the lock, facing inwards. The wooden baulks set diagonally across are to protect the paddle gear from damage when boats are waiting to use the lock.

34 There was a branch from the Thames and Severn Canal at Siddington into Cirencester, where th canal company had built a fair-sized basin. One of the most famous trips to be made over the Thames and Severn Canal was that of boatman Joseph Hewer, who originally came from Chalford. Owing to the state of the canal he had been forced to take his boats and move into the Swindon area Hearing that the Thames and Severn was opening again, he is reputed to have brought a cargo of 37 tons of coal from the Cannock Coalfields in Staffordshire to Cirencester in March 1904. It was the first water-borne coal to come to the wharf for 16 years. Whi it is known that barges traded over the Stroudwater and Thames and Severn Canals this picture is clearly of a narro boat, *The Staunch.* Yet it is reputed to have carried 37 tons, and that on a waterway which was not in particularl good condition. Normal loading for a horse-drawn narrow boat is 25 tons. I is known that he only owned one boat that time, as he had had to part with h other three boats before leaving Swindon.

33

35 Every canal wharf had to have its haulier; otherwise cargoes could not be shifted to and from their final destinations. Frank Gegg of Cirencester was no doubt typical. The Gegg family had various interests in Cirencester, and in 1889 Frank started a coal merchant's business on the canal wharf. While at first he most probably relied on water-borne coal, he soon had to find alternatives, and much of it must have come in by rail instead. He continued in business until 1921 and then probably sold out to a rival. It was under his initiative that the narrow boat *Staunch* brought the coal into Cirencester in 1904. Frank Gegg's favourite horse, Joey, is seen between the shafts in this photograph taken on the weighbridge on the wharf. The cart is typical of the type used by local delivery firms for coal and other relatively heavy goods.

36 This absolutely charming study shows the Thames and Severn Canal apparently full of water, but actually on its last legs. The date on the lock beam is 1904 and was presumably one of the last rebuilds to be undertaken by the trust. This lock at Chalford is Bell lock, and the next one is Red Lion lock. Few boats of any sort disturb the play of these Edwardian children. Temple Thurston sums it up: 'The whole way from Stroud upwards is almost deserted now. We only met one barge in the whole journey. An old lady with capacious barge bonnet was standing humming quietly to herself at the tiller. That was the only boat we found on those waters. The locks are, however, good; some of them have only just been made within the last few years. But the draft of water is bad; in some places we just floated, and no more.'

37 A view of the Thames and Severn Canal at Chalford Vale looking down on Red Lion lock from the east, with Sevill's or Clayfield Mill in the foreground, and Chalford Station in the distance. The canal is full of water and could, therefore, have been taken at any time between 1900 and 1917. For many years there were the remains of the abandoned narrow boat *Union* belonging to James Smart of Chalford, one of the last of the Thames and Severn/Stroudwater carriers. The boat was left derelict as the result of an accident in Bell lock in 1917. A boatman, bringing a load of coal up, left his boat in Bell lock and went off for a meal, presumably in the nearby Bell Inn. While away his craft sank. The load was eventually recovered and the boat towed to this spot above Red Lion lock, where it was left until about 1930. Although the last boat over the summit and through Sapperton tunnel is thought to have been in 1911, traffic continued on the lower reaches despite the virtual absence of maintenance staff east of Chalford after 1912. The accident referred to here was probably on one of the last trips up the valley.

38/39 Soon after Temple Thurston left the Stroudwater Navigation and joined the Thames and Severn Canal his journey, he met up with the dredging gang, although no reference it appears in his book *The Flower of Gloster*. The scene is recorded, however, in his own personal photograph album. Most forms of can maintenance were slow to adjust to an form of mechanisation and dredging was usually no exception. Charles Jones, clerk of works to the canal company in the 1830s was continually being told of the shallow state of the canal with 'horses straining their utmost with block and tackle, and rop breaking to get the boats through the mud. . . .' In 1832 improvements were put in hand, but without any waterborne form of dredging equipment. Charles Hadfield in his book *Canals of Southern England* quote from an ex-employee when he says th later they used a '. . . spoon or scoop dredge, formed of a leather bag on an iron ring at the end of a long pole, lowered over the side of the boat, dragged along the bottom and raised b a windlass. . . .' It is thought that approximately ½cwt of mud could be raised at one time by this method. These two photographs by Temple Thurston show the spoon dredger at work near Stroud. Gloucestershire County Council used a small steam bucket ladder-dredger called *Empress* when they ran the canal in the early 1900s.

40 One of the distinctive features of the Thames and Severn Canal were the watchmen's cottages. The best remembered were the five round houses at Chalford, Coates, Cerney Wick, Marston Meysey and Inglesham. No-one is quite sure why they were built to this shape and all five appear to have been built in 1790. This is the round house at Chalford, photographed in June 1937 after the canal had been closed. The picture was taken by a Great Western Railway photographer for one of their famous series of holiday posters, or even more likely for possible use as an illustration in a railway carriage. The round houses were for canal lengthsmen and toll keeper, who would have had a first-rate view of approaching traffic from the upstairs window. The ground floor with entrance from the back was for stabling. Living accommodation is on the ground floor level, and this can be seen from this front view with the bedroom above. The Company's Arms next door is reputed to date in part at least from the fifteenth century.

41 Brimscombe Port, situated 2½ miles above the junction with the Stroudwater Navigation, was the headquarters of the Thames and Severn Canal and a great transhipment port. From the River Severn up to Brimscombe the Stroudwater and the Thames and Severn Canals could take Severn trows and other boats up to 15ft wide. From this point on, although the locks became fractionally longer, they narrowed down to 11ft, which effectively restricted traffic to Thames Western barges, small trows and narrow boats. It also precluded narrow boats working in pairs as they could not get into the lock side by side. Many cargoes were split or transhipped at Brimscombe, and the main canal company offices were situated in the projecting section of the main building. The rest was warehouse space. Away to the right is an island wharf for the storage of coal. It was designed in this way with two removable bridge connections to cut down pilfering. The port was reputed to be able to hold 100 boats. The idea of having different gauges was to make transhipment necessary, hence bringing business to Brimscombe.

42 A much later view of Brimscombe Port from the other direction. The main offices and warehouses can be identified with the older print. The boat on the left is moored to the coal storage island, while opposite is the weigh dock (see Plate 43).

BRIMSCOMBE PORT.

To the Company of Proprietors of the Thames and Severn Canal Navigation

This Plate is respectfully inscribed by I & H S Storer

43

44

A boat-weighing machine was erected at Brimscombe in 1845 'To check frauds known to be practised by the boatmen', and was similar to the one at Midford on the Somersetshire Coal Canal, and the one illustrated elsewhere on the Glamorganshire Canal. In the first twelve months of its use it detected 1,267 tons of undisclosed cargo, which yielded tolls of £153 18s 4d. Considering the initial cost was £1,062 15s 11d, the resulting return was a good business investment. It is seen here being dismantled in June 1937. The dock area was later converted into a swimming pool, but the health authorities soon put a stop to this unauthorised use! There is a model of the weighing machine in Stroud Museum.

44 Like the wharf at Stony Stratford on the Buckinghamshire branch of the Grand Union (see Volume 1, Plate 116-118), the Thames and Severn Canal at Brimscombe had its ship builders. The Thames and Severn Canal Company had established its own barge-building yards at the Bourn, just above Brimscombe port, and the first two boats were made there in 1786. Later the yard was leased to the Gardiner family for the building of Stroud-type barges. In 1884 Edwin Clark started building boats nearby at Hyde Mill. Later the firm was taken over by Isaac Abdela and Mitchell Limited who had other ship-building interests in Manchester and Queensferry. They built all types of river craft for this country as well as abroad. Those which

could be taken out via the canal went that way, while others which could be broken down into smaller sections were floated down the Stroudwater and re-assembled on the Gloucester and Berkeley Ship Canal at Saul. The canal was kept open to this yard up to about 1933, and even after this date they actually moved one or two of their specially made craft down the abandoned canal. Here is one of three river steamers built for tropical South America between 1902 and 1905.

45 A very functional looking tug, built in 1908.

46 The steam tug *Nsaba* built for an overseas client, possibly Russian.

45

46

47 Stroud barges were developed for trading on the Stroudwater Navigation to Brimscombe port. They would also cross the River Severn to pick up cargoes of Forest of Dean coal at such places as Bullo Pill and Lydney. This is a demasted Stroud barge on the Stroudwater being hauled by three donkeys (six ears and at least ten legs can be seen!). On the Severn a Stroud barge could set a square sail. These craft were 68ft x 12ft 6in with a 50 ton capacity and were double ended. This one was probably owned by James Smart of Chalford, one of the last traders on the navigation. The photograph is thought to have been taken in the early 1930s when donkey or 'hanimal' towing was still quite common in this area. Note the swing bridge on the right of the picture. While the Stroudwater did not appear at first to be affected by railway competition, this gradually had its effect. The problem with the Thames and Severn's lack of water and subsequent lack of trade did not cause too much concern, as the Stroudwater got very little traffic from that canal. Trading ended in 1941 and the canal was officially abandoned in 1954. There are now active plans to revive both waterways.

48 Here is a very well kept narrow boat trading on the Stroudwater Navigation around 1910. It is seen passing the Midland Railway line near Stonehouse. Narrow boat *Pioneer* was owned by Charles Brayston of Gloucester. The traditional paintings on the cabin doors are there, as is the water can on the cabin roof, although there are no brass rings around the detachable chimney. The boat is returning empty after delivering a load of stone or coal, the side cloths are folded into the hold and the top planks laid along the top of it. The wheelbarrows are a reminder that the boatmen usually had to unload the cargoes themselves at country wharves. A twenty-five-ton loaded boat would take a two-man crew about half a day to unload.

49 One of the principle traffics acro the Bristol Channel to the Devon and Cornwall coasts was coal from South Wales. Similarly, higher up the estua of the River Severn, coal from the Forest of Dean was in great demand. This coal was shipped out from Lydn and Bullo Pill and in the main it came onto the canal system at Framilode, t entrance to the Stroudwater Navigation. In 1817, for example, 9,4 tons of coal came in at Framilode dur the first part of the year, all bound fo Brimscombe port. Of this, over half came from the Forest of Dean. This the entrance lock at Framilode photographed around 1900. The demasted trow *Irene* is waiting to pas through the lock into the River Sever Framilode was a small port in its own right, and in 1795 seven boats were registered here. On occasions schoon such as the *Chalie* and *Lane*, which ea carried 90 tons would come to Framilode from Newport with coal – they would unload half and continue Brimscombe with the remainder. Th craft on the bank to the left look like Stroud barges, open-holded craft wh could cross the Severn to Lydney or Bullo Pill.

47

50 There were four main Severnside ports, Lydney, Bullo Pill, Sharpness and Chepstow. Bullo Pill, seen here, was typical. Originally it consisted of tidal riverside wharves, but in 1818 the construction of a wet dock was commenced. As can be seen, coal was loaded into the boats in the dock by means of a coal drop. This photograph was taken in 1948 long after the area had been abandoned for trade and clearly shows the tidal wharves, dock gate and coal drop.

51 Another route built across part of Southern England was the Wilts and Berks Canal from Abingdon on the Thames to Semington on the Kennet and Avon Canal. It was not completed until 1810 at a cost of £250,000. If one looks on a map at the route taken by the Thames and Severn and the Kennet and Avon Canals, it is difficult to see why the Wilts and Berks was ever built at all. It passed mainly through agricultural land, and the chief towns on its route had a total population of only about 23,000 people in 1801. By far the largest was Swindon, but then it was a small town of 1,098 people, and of course, it expanded due to the railway, not the canal. It was a long canal, some 52 miles long, exclusive of branches to Wantage, Longcot, Calne and Chippenham. The peaceful scene shown in this beautifully detailed painting is the junction of the Wilts and Berks Canal with the River Thames at Abingdon.

52 One of the principle cargoes carried on the Wilts and Berks Canal was coal. In fact, one of the ideas behind the canal was to extend the ar in which coal from the Somerset pits could be sold. Once the canal opened however, it was found that the Somerset pits could not provide enou coal for those people who wanted it. One set of figures show that if the pit produced 2,020 tons in a week, 1,389 went down the Somersetshire Coal Canal but only 500 tons or so reachec the Wilts and Berks Canal. Problems with stoppages on the Somersetshire Coal Canal did not help either. The Wilts and Berks Canal was not a succ and only paid dividends to its shareholders for about ten years of its life around 1830. This peaceful scene painted at Stratton St Margaret whar in 1880 shows the canal well into decline.

50

53 The town of Wantage was one of the centres served by the canal. This is the town wharf, as photographed by Taunt in 1898. Despite the presence of the nearby Wantage Tramway, a good deal of traffic was carried over the one-mile Wantage branch. During the period 1893-6 1,327 tons of cargo (mainly coal) were carried by one trader, Hiskins and Sons from Semington and Wantage, and even more cargo (surprisingly) left Wantage for Abingdon. It is difficult to judge from this picture whether this Hiskins boat is waiting for a cargo or is in the first stages of decay. The last recorded traffic over the canal was in 1906, and it was officially closed in 1914.

54/55 One of the more unusual bridges in Swindon was the Golden Lion Bridge. In recent years a very skilled artist has painted a magnificen[t] mural of this lifting bridge on the side of a house in the town. The painting captures a lot of the feel of the period. In order that pedestrians would not b[e] inconvenienced when the bridge was raised, two footbridges were provided[.] Later, when the canal became disused and before the bridge was finally demolished and rebuilt, the footbridges were removed. The view down the street shows that the Swind[on] Tramway actually ran over the bridge as well. This picture could have been [as] late as 1910. It is interesting to note th[at] there would appear to be no protectio[n] for road users once the bridge was raised. Golden Lion bridge was a lift-bridge (similar to one at Preston on th[e] Lancaster Canal, Volume 1, Plate 113[)]. It was raised by hand power and help[ed] by counter-weights. Some of the mechanism is shown open on the painting, but enclosed by iron casting[s] on the photograph.

54

56 In 1819 a new canal was opened which it was thought would help the Wilts and Berks Canal. This was the North Wilts Canal, running from Swindon to Latton, near Cricklade, on the Thames and Severn Canal. This offered much easier access to coal from the Forest of Dean coming down the Thames and Severn onto the North Wilts and then onto the Wilts and Berks. Another great advantage was thought to be that through traffic for the Thames and London need not now traverse the upper reaches of that river, which was said to be in poor navigable condition, causing many delays to traffic. Like the Wilts and Berks, the North Wilts Canal suffered from railway competition, through traffic was not as high as expected, and anyway in later years the Thames and Severn had its own problems with lack of water and stoppages. This picture of Fleet Street Bridge in Swindon was taken around 1914, and shows the North Wilts Canal just before abandonment.

57 De Salis managed to navigate the Wilts and Berks Canal in 1895 but by the time he wrote his *Bradshaw*, published nine years later, he had to say 'although the canal is not officially closed, navigation throughout the whole of the system has practically ceased owing to the income being insufficient to meet the cost of maintenance.' The derelict state of the canal at the main wharf in Swindon is clearly shown in this photograph date 1914.

CANALS OF THE SOUTH WALES VALLEYS

hese waterways have been singled out because they are a
oup completely on their own — going down to the sea,
dmittedly, but unconnected with the rest of the system. The
ajority of the cargoes carried were the dirty, heavy ones of the
ndustrial Revolution — coal, iron and limestone. They all
ventually succumbed to the railways as each colliery and
orks became connected with the main lines. Once the valley
ilways were linked with the rest of the country, then their
roducts could be taken direct and not have to be shipped out
Cardiff, Neath, Newport, etc. Initially, of course, many
orse drawn tramroads connected the various works with the
anals.

The Welsh canals were hard work. They consisted of ladders
locks going upwards to the highest collieries and iron works
the valleys. There were thirty locks in seven miles on the
ain line of the Monmouthshire Canal, and another thirty-
o on its 10½-mile Crumlin branch. The Swansea Canal was
xteen miles long and had thirty-six locks. With some of these
aterways carrying over 200,000 tons of cargo a year, one
onders how many people were employed, not only boatmen,

but lock keepers, maintenance staff, toll collectors, boat
builders and repairers. In addition, of course, the number of
horses must also have been considerable.

Some idea of the financial problems of the Welsh canals can
be gained from figures published by Edwin Pratt covering the
half year ending 31 December 1905. The Monmouthshire
Canal received £866 in tolls and paid out £1,557 in expenses!
The Swansea Canal came a little nearer making ends meet with
tolls of £1,386 and expenses of £1,643. Of course, the
waterways were doing much better in the mid-nineteenth
century.

Particular attention has been paid in this section to give
details of the boats involved as they were unique on the British
canal scene, and very few survive. They are very reminiscent of
the mine boats used in the Duke of Bridgewater's mines at
Worsley. Under Great Western Railway ownership a number
of these were taken from the dying canals of Wales onto the
railway's Kennet and Avon Canal for use as maintenance
boats.

58 The boats on the South Wales
canals were some of the simplest on the
whole of the British canal system. As
the canals were not connected to other
waterways, there were no new
influences in their boat building, and
the boats stayed basically the same right
through the canals' lifetime. Wood was
the building material used; although
one or two metal ones were made, they
were not in general use. In 1893 the
Glamorganshire Canal built a steam
cargo-carrying tug of 20 ton capacity
called *Bute*, but this was not a success.
All South Wales boats had open holds
and a few which carried perishable
cargoes could be sheeted across, but as
most of the cargoes were mineral, this
was not generally necessary. All South
Wales boats were pointed at both ends,
though only Neath, Tennant and
Swansea boats could hang the helm on
either end. This photograph shows a
Monmouthshire Canal boat, 60ft long
by 8ft 6in beam, capacity 20 tons on a
draft of 2ft 9in. Boats on the
Monmouthshire, Brecon and
Abergavenny and Glamorganshire
Canals were fitted with cabins as on
occasions the crews did sleep on board.
Unlike the Midland narrow boats the
stove was at the fore end of the cabin
with the berths along each side. This is
Crindau Bridge, just north of Newport.

59 A Glamorganshire Canal boat, 60ft long by 8ft 6in beam, capacity 20 tons on a draft of 2ft 9in. These boats were very similar to the Monmouthshire Canal boat. The horse towing mast is approximately 6ft tall and is stepped vertically when the boat is loaded; but when unloaded, as in this picture, it would be sloped rearwards or sideways to avoid the low bridges. The scene is Ynysangharad locks, Pontypridd and is as late as the mid 1930s, although with the exception of the van it is almost timeless. The boatman has the horse's feeding bowl around his shoulders. The horse's fodder would have been carried under the deck forward.

60 A Neath and Tennant Canal boat, 60ft long by 9ft beam, carrying 24 tons on a draft of 2ft 9in. This boat is under repair in a Tennant Canal yard at Aberdulais. The South Wales boats were all constructed on narrow-boat principles using flat bottoms of elm, sides of oak and oak again for the knees. Nearly all boats had hefty rubbing strakes known as fenders.

61 A Neath and Tennant type boat showing the name carved into the top plank of the bow. The boatman with the horse is dressed in typical fashion, although it is fairly obvious that it is one of his bosses who is in the boat. The horse has no fancy harness or other decoration save for one brass on his forehead.

62 All dressed up for a special outing on the Monmouthshire Canal with both horse and boatman in untypical attire. The boatman has on his best suit with watch and chain, while the horse is bedecked with many brasses, a very ornate harness with decorated hames. The harness does not include the coloured wooden bobbins associated with some Midland canal horses. Instead here the chain passes through a leather pipe which stops it from chafing the horse's side. This, incidentally, was also the practice on the Leeds and Liverpool Canal. George Smith writing in *Our Canal Population* (1878) says of canal horses '. . . they are, as a rule, in the last stages of decay, and more fit for the knacker's yard than for work.' In another passage he says that it cost 1s 6d a day to keep a boat horse.

63/64 The Glamorganshire Canal was typical of the South Wales waterways. Opened in 1794, it was just over 24 miles long, and contained no less than forty-nine locks, falling nearl 550ft to the sea at Cardiff. It was built to serve the iron works around Merthy Tydfil. The canal held sway in the valley for over 60 years, carrying over 600,000 tons in one year in the 1850s. even competed successfully with the Taff Vale Railway for ten years withou any undue decrease in trade. There were problems, however, both with the management and the canal itself. Inevitably with such heavy lockage an high traffic density there were water shortages and congestion. As early as 1865 a short section of the canal at Merthyr Tydfil was abandoned, and then on 6 December 1898 the top thir was closed due to mining subsidence. Only the Cardiff to Pontypridd section was still active in 1915. These photographs dated 1908 show a total stoppage at Dynea just below Pontypridd due to a bank burst.

Glamorgan Canal
Denia
19 Octr 08.

63

64

65 Due to the stoppage shown in the previous photographs, essential canal borne supplies for Pontypridd had to be transferred to horse and cart for onward transmission by road. This is the wharf at Foundry Bridge Upper Boat. The craft in the foreground is a maintenance boat (it has no cabin) and is most probably loaded with materials to help with the repair of the canal breach. Although the trading boats had cabins, family boats were a great rarity, the crews living on land. Charles Hadfield in his *Canals of South Wales* says 'There were thought to be over 200 boats at work . . . the boats were not usually worked continuously, however, for most of the boatmen lived around Nantgarw and when it could be arranged they moored their boats near the village and went home.' The other boat is one from the Glamorganshire Canal Company's own carrying fleet.

66 Every canal exists on tolls from the craft using it to make itself an income. A canal would normally be divided into sections, often of different lengths, dependent on the terrain being covered. Normally a boat when it was new would be gauged by a company representative. Displacement would be measured empty and then at 2½cwt intervals until its normal trading capacity was reached. A copy of these dimensions would be given to each toll keeper, who then only had to gauge from the mark on the gunwale to water level to find out how much cargo was actually being carried. On the Glamorganshire Canal they had a more complicated system. The unladen weight of each boat was known, so the full boats were weighed on this gigantic weighing machine. The loaded boat came into a lock over which the machine was suspended, the water would be drained out and the boat would settle onto the pan of the scales. Because of the time taken to weigh boats by this method, it is thought to have been used only as a check when weight was in doubt. This relic, which survived in the centre of Cardiff well into the 1950s, has subsequently been taken down and re-erected at the Waterways Museum, Stoke Bruerne, over a disused Grand Junction lock

fitted with gates from the Montgomeryshire Canal, and displayed weighing a Midlands type narrow boat. There were two other such weighing machines on British Canals, one at Midford on the Somersetshire Coal Canal, and the other on the Thames and Severn Canal.

67 One of the factories served by the Glamorganshire Canal was the chain works of Brown Lennox Ltd, Pontypridd, seen here in 1890. About 80yd above the top gates of this two-rise staircase lock the canal water entered the top basin of the works and was used to drive waterwheels which worked the chainmaking machinery. The canal boats brought in coal and finished iron from Merthyr Tydfil. The canal water flowed away under the chain works proving-room into the bottom basin. Two boats are berthed in this basin waiting for loads of chain to be sent to the official proving house in Cardiff. The outlet is below the lower lock.

65

68

69

70

Svedenstjerna, who was an early
ᵼustrial spy, commented in his *Tour
reat Britain, 1802-3, '. . . at
ᵼydarren alone there are three blast
ᵼnaces, three refineries, twenty-five
ᵼdling and eight bloom-furnaces,
ᵼh the necessary hammers and rolling
ᵼls, as well as nine or ten steam
ᵼines . . . it is said that the number of
ᵼkers in all the works runs to about
ᵼ00 . . . besides a number of smaller
ᵼways, on which coal and ironstone is
ᵼught to the blast furnaces, Mr.
ᵼmfray has laid down a large one for
ᵼ transport of bar iron which runs for
ᵼrly seven Swedish quarter miles
ᵼse to the Cardiff canal.' Ironically, it
ᵼs on this very tramway that
ᵼvithick tested his first locomotive on
ᵼFebruary 1804. This boat is not
ᵼded with bar iron, coal or any other
ᵼduct of the Industrial Revolution.
ᵼas just emerged from Lock Lewis
ᵼ crew have left the gates open in
ᵼ working boat manner) in the
ᵼmer of 1908. Although it is not a
ᵼily boat there is a lady on board, so
ᵼsumably this was some form of joy
ᵼ. At one time, the Swansea Canal
ᵼally had a ruling which enjoined
ᵼ 'no females be allowed to navigate
ᵼges'.

69 In the early 1900s a writer in J.
Lloyd's *The History of the Old South
Wales Iron Works* commented '. . . to
my surprise, it had fallen into complete
disuse, not a vestige of a canal boat was
to be seen, and the water supply turned
off into the river! Very little more than
one hundred years have been long
enough to bring about this marvellous
change from high dividends and great
prosperity to absolute ruin . . . and on
the day of my visit the water in the lock
was green and stagnant and the massive
lock gates had not apparently turned
upon their hinges for months past! . . .'
He was referring to the Abercynon to
Merthyr section of the Glamorganshire
Canal. This photograph was taken
about this time at the picturesque
North Road Lock (No 49) in Cardiff.
This thatched lock house appears on a
number of local picture postcards. The
horse is about to take up the strain as
the boat comes under the bridge and
into the open canal, the towing mast
having been lent over to avoid the arch
of the bridge, similar to Birmingham
day-boat practice. Are the children on
the right playing cricket? It looks very
much like it!

70 The Glamorganshire Canal below
Pontypridd remained in being until
1942, when the last trading boat passed
down the length, for on 25 May there
was a breach at Nantgarw which was
never repaired. The remaining
southern part of the canal was
purchased by the Cardiff City Council.
Here we see the Lord Mayor and
Councillors early in 1944, studying the
waterway that they have bought. They
had also bought the railway which
belonged to the canal company, the
locomotive seen here was called
Delwyn, and was the canal company's
last steam locomotive.

71 This Sunday School outing took place in the early 1900s and is at Glyntaf, Pontypridd. The boat is absolutely typical of craft on this waterway. The outing depicted here is not so lavishly organised as was one by the Rector of Camerton (Somerset) in 1823: 'Having engaged one of the coal barges, I had it fitted up for the ladies with an awning and matting against the sides, and tables and chairs from the public house. . . .'

72 The Aberdare Canal was opened in 1812 to connect with the Glamorganshire Canal at Abercynon. Its original purpose was to transport iron down from the flourishing ironworks, but this traffic dropped off almost as soon as the canal was opened. Later, in the 1840s, a number of collieries producing steam coal for industry and railways were sunk in the area and trade flourished again. By the end of this decade it was carrying 160,000 tons a year. This traffic caused water problems and a pumping engine had to be installed to raise water from the River Cynon, this installation, incidentally, was being financed by the Glamorganshire Canal as they eventually got the water. Railway competition finally overtook the Aberdare Canal, and in 1900 it closed. This photograph was taken a few years later and depicts the former head of the canal, which was situated between the village of Cwmbach and Aberdare. The crane is unusually sturdily built, presumably to cope with the heavy cargoes associated with the iron industry or the moving of containers of coal from railway wagons to the canal boats.

73 The Swansea Canal obtained its Act of Parliament in 1798 and was completed by 1804. It ran for 15 miles down the Tawe Valley and included in its length thirty-six locks. It was a profitable canal, right from the time of its opening until 1895, and in its best years carried nearly 400,000 tons per annum. This is a somewhat romanticised view looking south towards Swansea around 1860, with the canal in the foreground. The Landore viaduct carried the South Wales Railway (amalgamated with the GWR in 1863) across the valley of the River Tawe between Landore and Llansamlet. The River Tawe was tidal at this point and sailing vessels carrying copper ore to the quays above Landore would have used the opening span of the viaduct. The viaduct was designed by Isambard Kingdom Brunel in 1850 — it was 1,788ft long, and ran at a height of 88ft over the water. It was demolished in 1887, and rebuilt in 1889.

71

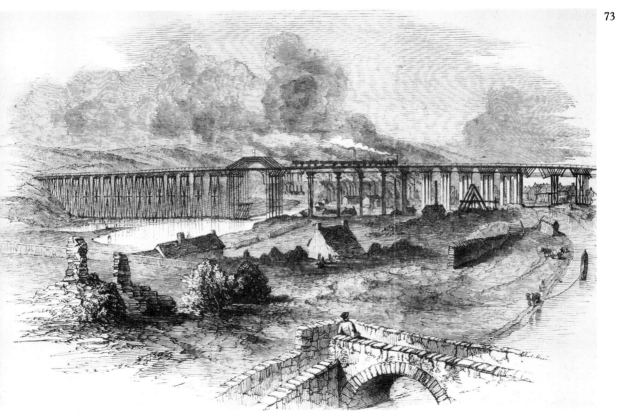

74

75

The Neath Canal is 13 miles long and contains some nineteen locks in its run from Glyneath down through the town of Neath itself to the quays at Giants Grave and Briton Ferry. At first the railway competition stayed on the other side of the valley, but slowly the major collieries and works were connected to it. The canal paid its final dividend in 1896, and by 1907 the weight carried was down to 11,000 tons per annum. It is thought that the last commercial boat, a market boat, ran in 1916. This photograph was taken in 1914 at a time when the canal was on its last legs and shows the junction with the Tennant Canal at Aberdulais. The Tennant Canal swings right under Pontgam (the crooked bridge), while the Neath Canal continues southwards to go under the Vale of Neath railway line from Aberdare.

75 A boatyard on the Tennant Canal at Aberdulais in 1914. The Tennant Canal is on the left and the Neath Canal on the right. By the bridge are two typical South Wales boats. The larger one is a standard 20-ton day boat while the other is a shorter boat built to take ten tons only and used mainly for maintenance and repair work. As this is so late in the canal's life, it is thought that the boat in the dock is under repair or may even have been left there and abandoned. The canal was closed to commercial traffic a few years after this picture was taken, but amazingly the canal company decided it needed a new maintenance boat in the 1930s and in 1934 carpenter Ben Jones built such a boat from scratch at Tonna. It was called the *Ivy May*.

76 George Tennant built the tidal dock system with extensive wharves on the east side of the Tawe estuary opposite to Swansea, and called it Port Tennant. To feed these docks, he took over the Glan-y-Wern Canal and cut the Red Jacket Canal. In 1824 he extended these to make a canal 8½ miles long to join the Neath Canal at Aberdulais. The disadvantage with Port Tennant as built was that it could only take smaller coasting craft and at low tide they had to lie on the mud. In 1881 the Prince of Wales Dock was built with access from the canal. Kings Dock was opened in 1909 and this photograph of it, taken in June 1931, shows the very end of the Tennant Canal alongside this new dock. The Prince of Wales (or East) Dock, the Kings Dock and the Queens Dock all became Great Western Railway property, though the Tennant Canal remained in private hands.

79

77 The Tennant Canal still remains in family ownership although commercial traffic on it ceased in 1934. It is now kept open as an industrial water supply and serves a great variety of industry along its banks. There is now a scheme afoot to restore the Neath and Tennant Canals. This photograph shows a group of boatmen at Swansea bridges between Dynevor Swing Bridge and Jersey Marine in 1912. The bridge over carried the Rhondda and Swansea Bay Railway, while in the background can just be seen the earlier competitor, the Vale of Neath Railway.

78 The Monmouthshire Canal was conceived in 1792 and mostly completed by 1796. It served two valleys running north from Newport. The main line went north to Pontypool, paralleling the River Usk for a short distance, whilst the main branch went away to the left following the River Ebbw to Crumlin. The seals of the company are interesting, and this one shows a highly stylised view of the ruined Newport Castle with the River Usk in the foreground and presumably the branches and foliage coming from the top of the battlements showing the ruined nature of the building. The horse is towing a very non-committal boat. At the time the seal was designed the canal had not been built, so the engraver had not actually seen a boat on it! Behind the canal is the basin of the Port of Newport with the Welsh hills beyond.

79 In 1845 the canal obtained a bill to enable it to become a railway company and in 1848 this new company had its own seal. Dennis Hadley in his book *Waterways Heraldry* describes it as 'typical of mid nineteenth century ecclesiastical gothicism'. Unusually both the canal boat and the railway locomotive are good representations of their subjects. The motto translates as 'quickly and securely'.

80 Engineered by Thomas Dadford Junior, the Crumlin branch of the Monmouthshire Canal had thirty-two locks grouped together in flights. It was just over ten miles long. The first flight was at Allt-yr-ynn (the declivity of the ash trees), a local beauty spot favoured by picture postcard photographers in the earliest days of this century. Many locals knew this area as Little Switzerland. So that the boats could pass through the locks in the minimum amount of time, the top gates have a gate paddle as well as the normal two side paddles. Did picture postcard photographers take around with them groups of children dressed in their Sunday best; such groups are often found in the foreground of their pictures?

81 The fourteen locks at High Cross, Rogerstone, lifted the Crumlin Branch canal over 150ft, and were built as a staircase with a passing pound in the middle. Their similarity is more with Bratch than Foxton as the chambers are separated by about 20ft and do not have common gates. This is clearly shown in this photograph. This lock, Number 5, was sometimes known as the sea lock because of its peculiar shape. Some historians claim that the top of the chamber was widened to act as a passing place for boats but this seems unlikely as there is a passing pound already provided in the flight. A much more likely theory is that it allowed a greater volume of water to descend the flight to a deeper lock further down.

82 The dramatic Crumlin railway viaduct was built by Liddel and Gordon to carry the Taff Vale extension of the Newport, Abergavenny and Hereford railway over Ebbw Valley and in so doing it also crossed the upper reaches of the Crumlin Branch. Completed in 1857, the viaduct was the largest in the world for many years. It had a total length of 1,650ft and the tracks crossed 210ft above the valley. Both railway and canal became part of the Great Western Railway undertaking, and this picture shows a train of thirty-one assorted wagons rumbling across the viaduct behind one of the once ubiquitous GWR 'Dean Goods' 0-6-0 tender engines. Eventually, like the canal, the railway was closed and the viaduct was dismantled in 1965, leaving only The Viaduct public house to indicate that it had ever existed.

83 One of the major cargoes of the Monmouthshire Canal was bricks, as there were a number of brickworks along its route. One of the principal ones was at Allt-yr-ynn on the Crumlin arm just above the picturesque flight of locks, and a mile from the junction with the Pontypool section. This photograph is thought to have been taken around 1914; it shows one boat loaded and ready to go with a horse standing on the tow path, while an empty boat waits to pull in against the pile of bricks and pipes to be loaded. This brick works closed in 1924.

84 The Brickworks wharf in Newport was situated next to the Corde Dos Na Works. Many readers will have seen a well-known photograph of a coal boat approaching a double drawbridge at Newport. The Brickworks wharf is just up the canal from this drawbridge. The railway lines that crossed that drawbridge lead to the sidings seen in this photograph. The bricks have come from the Allt-yr-ynn brickworks, and the date is thought to be 1914. Like the wharf crane in the previous picture, this one has been especially adapted to load bricks.

83

85 In the 1840s the canal was worried by the threat of railway competition and obtained an Act to turn itself into a railway company as well. The Monmouthshire Railway and Canal opened its own line, the Newport and Pontypool Railway, in March 1853. Slowly traffic left the canal, and in August 1875 the railway lines were leased to the Great Western Railway, who took them over completely in 1880. The first few years of the MR & CC were unhappy ones, as the work of re-laying feeder tramroads and plate ways and turning them into railways to take locomotives was often delayed and there were many mechanical disasters. 1930 saw the last cargo carried on the Crumlin branch canal while traffic continued spasmodically on the main line until 1938. The Crumlin branch was closed in 1949 and the main line abandoned in 1962. Here at a spot north of Cwmbran station the MR & CC line from Newport to Pontypool ran alongside the canal. This photograph, taken in 1912, shows the canal company's dredger hard at work. In the background is a 'Dean Goods' 0-6-0. One well-known writer on the South Wales canals when shown this photograph remarked 'Did the Great Western Railway *really* dredge the Monmouthshire Canal in 1912? I can scarcely believe it!' Here is the proof that they did. Perhaps it was preventative maintenance or was it a publicity stunt for Priestmans, the dredger manufacturers — as this picture does appear in their brochure!

86 Even though the Crumlin branch had not been used commercially since 1930, it still had to be maintained. In February 1946 it burst its banks at Abercarn, 2½ miles down from the head of navigation at Crumlin, and close to Abercarn colliery. These photographs were taken by a railway photographer on 22 February 1946, a few days after the breach had occurred. The breach was repaired, but the canal finally closed in 1949.

87 Some boats from the South Wales Canals found their way onto the Kennet and Avon Canal. As traffic declined in Wales, a fleet of these boats were sent over to Berkshire in the 1920s. As the Kennet and Avon was controlled by the Great Western Railway, most of the boats were transported by rail, and were off-loaded at Thatcham. Because of complaints about the condition of the canal, the Great Western Railway was forced into making improvements in the late '20s and early '30s, and bought a number of new dredgers. The majority of the boats from South Wales were to be used as mud boats in connection with these improvements. Here is a boat from the Brecon and Abergavenny Canal or Monmouthshire Canal outside the former warehouse alongside the east side of the southern end of the south basin at Newbury Wharf around 1930.

88/89 Very little is known about these two photographs. They were obtained together, mounted in a frame, and could be a Church or Sunday School outing, both taken in one year, maybe a year separated them, or perhaps two different boats on one trip. It is thought that the date is around 1912. The place could be Griffithstown, near Pontypool. It is absolutely amazing the number of people that can be crammed into a working boat when they are used for pleasure purposes. The Board of Trade would not like it nowadays! The last known Sunday School outing by boat in South Wales is thought to have been in 1946 when the Pontypool Salvation Army hired two Great Western Railway boats for a horsedrawn journey from Pontymoile basin to Goytre.

DOWN TO THE SEA

The waterways in this section are probably more varied than in any other. These were canals built for the specific purpose of either sending some product down to the coast for export or the specific import of another. Because it was not possible to connect these canals to the main inland waterway network, they developed along their own local lines and used boats which were most likely unique to their own waterways.

Some canals in this category went from harbours where coasting vessels could load direct into the canal craft, such as at Bude, Bridgwater or Southampton. The latter, of course, catered for trade from overseas as well. The Parliamentary Act for the Bude Canal actually stipulates that the harbour had to be improved as part of the whole plan. The canals at Carlisle and Ulverston were ship canals and were built purely to allow coastal vessels to reach towns without unloading, and the Chichester section of the Portsmouth and Arundel also came into this category, creating inland ports.

This section also includes one or two river navigations. After all, rivers were the first waterways to be made navigable and a number of them fell into disuse with the coming of canals. The River Severn is one which has always amazed the author, as having been navigable so far upstream by comparison with present-day conditions. Here, possibly, is a waterway one is glad is not being restored above Stourport, as somehow fibreglass cruisers or even narrow boats on the river at Coalport and under the Iron Bridge itself would be incongruous.

90

90 The canal at Bude was always intended to serve the agricultural interests of the area. The north Devon and Cornwall coastal lands were in the main heavy and acid, and one way of rendering them more fertile was to treat them with sea sand. It so happened that the sand at Bude had a high calcium carbonate content. While the sand could be collected free of charge, it was the transport inland that was so difficult. The original Act for a canal to be built inland from Bude was passed through Parliament in 1774, but it was not until 1819 that work started; it was completed in 1825. The canal was 35½ miles long in all, and was divided into three branches to Tamar Lake (a water feeder), Blagdon Moor Wharf (near Holsworthy) and Druxton (near Launceston). In the final Act the sum of £4,618 was allowed for improvement to the already existing small harbour at Bude. These improvements were very necessary as it was extremely treacherous trying to get a sailing vessel into the harbour due to insufficient protection. This photograph, taken on 17 September 1929, long after the canal had closed, shows the ketch *Ceres* leaving Bude harbour, possibly returning to one of the South Wales ports for a cargo of coal. Behind the ship can be seen the rail of a small bridge. This formed part of the horse-drawn railway which still took sand from the shore up to the dockside.

91 Most of the waterway was built as a tub-boat canal taking boats 20ft by 5ft 6in. These boats were horse-drawn and made up into small trains. One of the features of the canal was the six inclined planes. An unusual aspect of the design of the tub boats was that they had wheels fixed to them which ran on the rails of the inclined planes, thus doing away with the need for a carrying cradle. A Bude tub boat is now on show at the Exeter Maritime Museum. This scene, around 1890, shows tub boats awaiting their cargo at Bude harbour. The ketch *Stuckley*, registered at the North Cornwall port of Padstow, has quite likely brought in a cargo of coal from South Wales, probably Mumbles. Certainly in December 1880 she had such a cargo on board when the ship was temporarily wrecked on Bude breakwater. *Stuckley* was built in 1839 and had a carrying capacity of 32 tons. By 1883 she was owned by George Barrett of Bude.

92 Below the Marhamchurch inclined plane at the head of the barge canal was Helebridge Wharf, seen here. Barges used to bring coal and sand up to the wharf where some of it was kept (hence the warehouses) and sold in the local area. The rest would have been transferred into tub boats for onward transmission. Tub boats bringing cargoes down the canal would not have normally unloaded here. They would have gone on down the barge canal to the harbour to load directly into ships moored there. The tub boat at the wharf-side is interesting for its conventional bow — most tub boats were, of course, square ended. A similar type of boat is known to have worked on the nearby Torrington Canal. The boat with the bow would have been placed at the head of a train of boats, the bow making them swim and steer better, and facilitating horse towage. Dummy bows are placed on the trains of 'Tom Puddings', or compartment boats, still used on the Aire and Calder Navigation for the same reasons — though these are towed by a tug. The derrick on the wharf looks as if it has come from a ship.

93 While maintenance on the Bude Canal had been generally good, trade gradually declined after the mid 1870s. In 1891 the canal was finally closed. The problem had been that it never attracted the expected amount of trade. Something like 300,000 tons a year had been forecast, but in fact 59,620 tons was the highest recorded figure, and at the time of closure it was down to 22,315 tons. Sea sand had always been the staple cargo, followed by a fairly regular 2,000-4,000 tons of coal carried inland each year. As the canal never actually reached either Holsworthy or Launceston it is likely that the coal was for villages along the canal side. Had the canal reached either of these towns then possibly the story of the Bude Canal might well have been prolonged. This picture was taken a few years after the canal had closed and shows the foot of the Marhamchurch incline, the second largest plane on the canal, which raised the waterway 120ft and was 836 long. The power for this incline, as with most of the others on the canal, was provided by a massive 50ft diameter overshot waterwheel. Amazingly it only took five minutes to raise one boat containing 4 tons of cargo to the top of the plane. Officially the two miles of canal below the Marhamchurch inclined plane did not close until 1924, but it looks almost un-navigable and low in water when this picture was taken.

92

94 The bottom two miles of the Bude Canal from the harbour to Marhamchurch inclined plane were built to barge canal specifications, 63ft by 14ft 7in. This stretch of waterway included two locks at Whalesborough and Rodds Bridge. The purpose of the larger section of canal was to allow certain ships and barges up to Helebridge basin, without the need for transhipment. Originally all such movement was conducted by horses but in 1860 Mr S. Smith of London, a shareholder in the canal company, purchased a steam boat to tow barges and tub boats over the lower section of the canal. It also acted as a harbour tug, assisting vessels in and out of the sea lock, but it was found to be uneconomic in operation. Its wash also damaged the canal banks, so it was soon sold. It is seen here outside the Falcon Hotel, Bude.

95 Ball clay is of high bulk and weight in proportion to its actual value, which means that transportation costs represent an unusually large share of its purchase price. Overland transport to the clay cellars or the dockside was expensive, so in 1792 James Templar, the landowner, opened the Stover Canal from Jetty Marsh on the River Teign to Ventiford nearly two miles away. In the early days the Teign barges were bow hauled down the canal as it was impossible to tow on the River Teign. The boats relied on the ebb and flow of the tides plus their single square sail. This is a typical group of Teign barges at Teigngrace in late 1937 waiting to be loaded from the clay cellars on the right. The barges were 50ft long by 14ft beam, and could load 25 tons each. Although the railway on the right took a lot of the trade, clay boats used the canal until 1939. All were unrigged by this time. The barge in the foreground of the photograph was named *George V* and was owned by Watts, Blake and Bearne, whose barges were distinguished by white gunwales.

96 In later years the boats were hauled by tugs, the first a steam tug called *Kestrel*. Later a local yard built tug with a Kelvin paraffin engine, which continued in service until the end of trading. Her name was *Heron*. *Heron* is seen here with a tow on the river reaches below the canal entrance lock at Jetty Marsh. One of the most interesting projects associated with the Stover Canal was the Hay Tor granite tramway. George Templar built a tramroad using granite rails laid as a plateway, from the granite quarries around Hay Tor down to the canal at Ventiford. It was opened in 1890. While large contracts were obtained for the stone, the various transhipments from wagon to canal to ships, and so on proved expensive. The tramway was closed by 1858 and this particular trad lost.

1790 ?

95

97   The River Tamar had been navigable up to the small settlement of Morwellham since the twelfth century, and even though the terrain was difficult it had served the inland town of Tavistock. With the growth of mining in the area, a canal was devised linking the town with the quay. This involved a tunnel, an aqueduct and an inclined plane! The promoters also hoped that they might strike rich veins of copper, tin lead or other minerals as they dug the tunnel, but this did not happen. The Tavistock canal was finally opened in June 1817. 'A numerous company of between 300 and 400 persons, in boats constructed of sheet iron, proceeded through the tunnel, a distance of a mile and three quarters, underground, beneath a canopy of solid rock, at the depth of 450 feet from the summit of the hill, accompanied in their dark passage by songs and music.. . .' This report says the boats were made of metal, but there is proof that the first boats were made of wood, and that metal ones did not come in until the late 1820s. These were shaped like tub boats and could load, on average, 4½ tons. Each was fitted with four wheels and could be used as a railway wagon on the inclined plane or

at the quayside. This is a very early picture, and is thought to have been taken in 1868, four years before the canal finally closed. The view is of Morwellham quay with the River Tamar in the foreground. The Tavistock Canal runs parallel with the skyline at top right, and the inclined plane to the quays is in the centre. Once the boats reached the base of the incline, they were railed diagonally right to the company's quays on the right-hand side of the picture. The other incline running from the top of the hillside to the left of the canal incline is that of the Devon Great Consols Mineral Railway. Note the great mounds of copper ore awaiting transhipment. In 1901 the pumps at the Devon Great Consols Mine finally ceased pumping—the mining boom was over, and Morwellham, as a port, was dead.

98   This photograph, taken in 1903, shows empty quays and the docks slowly silting up.

97

Morwellham

TAVISTOCK CANAL.

Persons desirous of Tendering for the undermentioned Work in connection with the Tavistock Canal:

1st.—To keep in repair the Railway on the Inclined Plane at Morwellham and all Machinery thereto belonging, as well as the Waggons used on the said Railway, and to keep the Towing Path leading from the Tunnel end to the top of the Inclined Plane.

2nd.—To keep in repair the Towing Path and Banks of the Canal, as well as the Locks, Hatches, and Wooden Bridges between the Tavistock Wharf and the Tunnel's mouth;

Are requested to send in Tenders to Mr. H. GILL, on or before Friday, the 22nd December instant.

DATED DECEMBER 15TH, 1854.

G. SPENCER, Printer, Bookseller, &c., Higher Market Street, TAVISTOCK.

99 Boats were normally towed along the canal by horse and then legged or poled through the tunnel. This does not seem to have been completely satisfactory, so various ideas were tried for speeding up the traffic flow. Steam haulage by rope and cable was suggested, but not implemented. Twin waterwheels, one at each end of the tunnel, hauling on a wire rope, were in operation in 1860, but they resulted in damage to the walls of the tunnel, presumably caused by scoring of the walls by the rope. The seasonal record for the canal, reached in 1837, was 20,009 tons carried, but after that trade declined. The Taunton and South Devon Railway opened in 1859, and took a lot of the traffic coming inland to Tavistock, and in the summer of 1872 the canal closed. The canal is still very much in existence today, as its waters have been harnessed to operate a small hydro-electric power station at Morwellham. The quays and inclines, etc, are all being conserved and the whole area is now part of the Morwellham Quay Open Air Museum.

100 The Bridgwater and Taunton Canal was an important one. Opened finally in 1827, it connected the town of Taunton to the River Parrett at Huntworth close by Bridgwater. In turn, the Parrett connected with the sea. Also bringing trade into Taunton for onward transmission was the Chard Canal — and of course the Grand Western for a few years, as well. Under the section on the Grand Western (Volume 1, Plates 60-3) there is mention of the canal which would have connected Taunton to Topsham and the River Exe, so cutting across the south-western peninsula. Had this happened, then of course the Taunton and Bridgwater Canal would have been part of it and have become even more important. In 1841 the Bridgwater and Taunton was extended a mile around Bridgwater and a new enclosed dock built to take coasting craft. The wharves and lock at Huntworth were then closed. This is the new dock at Bridgwater, around the turn of the century, packed with mainly top sail schooners and a brig. *Champion* built in 1853 at Bristol to carry 68 tons, and owned by J.C. Hunt of Bridgwater is in the foreground. *Champion* was a ketch-rigged trow, and would have probably traded down from the Bristol area or have come with coal from a Severn-side wharf. The one unusual vessel not featured in this picture, is the Brunel-designed steam dredger, commissioned in 1844, presumably as it was found that the new dock was silting up rapidly. This dredger operated until 1971 when it was taken overland to the Exeter Maritime Museum for preservation. The Brunel dredger was in reality an aquatic bulldozer, as it pushed silt along the bottom and left it where the current would carry it away.

101 The first lock away from Taunton is Firpool where the canal leaves the River Tone. At this point a weir was thrown across the river and controlled by sluices to make sure there was adequate water in the navigation into the town as well as controlling floodwater. Firpool lock was obviously a place where you could hire out a rowing boat and the small steam powered launch is interesting. The date is thought to be 1910. The canal was bought by the Great Western Railway in 1866 for £64,000. It would appear that the railway company let it decline as complaints were received from around 1870 onwards as to its condition. Commercial traffic stopped

around the turn of the century although other photographs show that the locks were kept in good order for some years after that.

102 Just below Firpool lock the Bridgwater and Taunton Canal passed close to the Great Western Railway locomotive depot and sidings. Canal water was pumped up into the large water tank, on top of the building on the left. The craft on the left look remarkably like iron tub boats, but are maintenance boats, while the hulk on the right is all that is left of one of the barges that used to trade on the canal. The other boat is an interesting one, being a mobile pump for canal use, to pump out lock chambers during repairs, flooded works, etc. It looks so much like a locomotive type boiler that one wonders if it was built at Swindon. Note the GWR tarpaulins covering the pump machinery.

103 Until Sidney Ashford publishes his definitive book on the Itchen Navigation, a number of questions relating to its history will remain unanswered. The River Itchen running inland from Southampton was reputed to have been navigable to Winchester before 1189, as at that time Godfrey de Lucy, Bishop of Winchester, is said to have restored the navigation. It is thought that the navigation was again improved in about 1710 and between 1767 and 1795. At its lower end at Wood Mill there was a sea lock connecting the navigation to the Itchen river and two miles further down the estuary were the Company's wharves at Northam. This photograph, taken around 1910, is thought to show the remains of Stoke Lock, which, when originally built, was turf-sided, strengthened with timber. The original of this photograph is entitled 'The Bargebank'. The navigation was locally known as the Barge river. The River Itchen was often termed 'The Old Barge' and the navigation sometimes known also as 'The New Barge'.

103

104 The Itchen Navigation fell approximately 100ft in its 10⅜ mile length and had fifteen locks, which meant that many of them were not particularly deep. Catherine Hill Lock seen here is one such and it is the first lock on the navigation from the Winchester end. In 1796 plans were mooted for joining the Itchen Navigation to the Basingstoke Canal, which would have given Southampton an inland route to London. Nothing came of this, and in 1840 the London and Southampton Railway was opened. The navigation's receipts were at this time £1,820 16s, but by the early 1860s were down to only £430 5s. In 1863 the navigation had three full-time employees: a Mr Clark as manager (ex-Southampton and Andover Canal, which had recently closed), a carpenter and a lock keeper. The last boat is reputed to have traded to Winchester in January 1896.

104

05 This is the head of navigation in Winchester at Blackbridge wharf. The far bridge is the stone Blackbridge while the nearest is Wharfbridge. In the background of the wharf area is another wharf called Scard's Wharf, named after Henry Scard, a barge owner trading on the navigation. The building at the back of the wharf is the old office building of the proprietors of the Itchen Navigation. The buildings in front were the wharf warehouses. Winchester Cathedral is visible above the trees. This navigation, never successful, could not compete with either railway competition or the local turnpike roads. Roads between two places such as Southampton and Winchester would have been in reasonable order in the early 1800s, and could have taken a lot of traffic from the waterway. Squabbling and law-suits behind the scenes did not help either. As a footnote, this navigation still looks in good heart because parts of it, like the long defunct Andover Canal, have been preserved for angling.

Black Bridge, Winchester,

106 An interesting but fanciful view of Blackbridge, Winchester, showing a loaded barge approaching the bridge with the wharf behind. The design of the boat is interesting, it has a swim-headed bow, like a punt. It has no provision for sails so must have been quanted by manpower or towed by men or horse. The canal Act had specified a horse path. There is no sign of either form of haulage in the picture. The cover at the rear of the barge is very much like that of a covered wagon. Paintings or artist's impressions can at times confuse the historian more than help him, and this is a good example of such confusion.

107 It had long been the intention to try and link London with the south coast by canal to avoid the dangerous sea routes around the Kent coast, and the problems in the Channel in times of war with France. Eventually, London was linked with Portsmouth, but it came too late, as the railway era was about to commence. The waterways consisted of the Wey and Arun Junction Canal (opened in 1816), the River Arun Navigation, and the Portsmouth and Arundel Canal (opened 1823). Also involved were the Chichester and Portsea Ship Canals, opened in 1822. Very few pictures seem to survive of the Wey and Arun Junction Canal when it was actually in use. This photograph, by Francis Frith, from a postcard, was taken 35 years after closure, and shows Rowner lock bottom gates near Billingshurst. Even though the canal was closed it was obviously not forgotten locally and as a local feature it was depicted derelict on a number of picture postcards such as this. The canal is now under active restoration.

108

8 Just as this volume was going press this picture turned up, ptioned 'Wey and Arun Canal, Lock Billingshurst'. A quick check with me members of the Wey and Arun anal Trust failed to gain a positive entification, though it was suggested at it might be a lock at Bramley, but inted in reverse. The two men working e lock look too smart for working atmen, so perhaps they are pleasure aters. It seems unlikely that the cture is of J.B. Dashwood who took e sailing craft *Caprice* through the anal in 1868, as his companion was a -year-old bargee. The picture shows e canal in the last throes of decay before sing. The lock gates do not look too fe while the beams are in a very poor te. The paddle on the right is raised, d the whirlpool in the water shows at it is working.
ugh McKnight collection.)

109 The next waterway in the chain from London to Portsmouth was the Portsmouth and Arundel Canal, which opened fully in 1823. The course was basically due west from Ford, some two miles below Arundel on the River Arun. It joined the Chichester branch and continued to the Chichester channel at Birdham. The canal Act of 1818 allowed for the Chichester branch to be built to ship canal size. Barges then entered the salt water of Chichester Harbour, rounding the north of both Thorney Island and Hayling Island by an especially dredged channel to enter Portsea Island via a ship canal at Milton. Traffic between London and Portsmouth never reached a tenth of its predicted amount, so this section of the through route was doomed almost from the outset. In 1847 it ceased to be commercially used but it was not officially liquidated until 1894. This canal bridge at Yapton was still standing in 1905 when this photograph was taken.

109

Old Canal Bridge Yapton

110 The section of the canal leading inland from Birdham to Chichester still continued to carry trade. This canal was of course made famous by Turner's painting, Chichester Canal, which shows a barque of the type which regularly used the waterway. Trade had gradually declined and figures show only 704 tons carried in 1898, not a very economical proposition. The last recorded traffic was a cargo of shingle delivered to Chichester basin in 1906. In 1924 the waterway was blocked by the lowering of two bridges; it was finally abandoned in 1928. Back in 1897 a light railway had been built from Chichester to Pagham harbour and Selsey. Called the 'Hundred of Manhood and Selsey tramway' it continued to operate until 1935 when it finally succumbed to the omnibus and private car. When it was constructed there was still trade on the Chichester Canal, and this bridge was built to carry the tramway over the waterway. Here, then, is a ketch about to negotiate the bridge. By the new state of the works, one gets the impression that this photograph was most likely taken very soon after the opening of the line in 1897.

111 Priestley described the Sankey Brook Navigation thus: 'this canal, was the first executed in the country, commenced in the River Mersey, at the mouth of Sankey Brook, from which it derives its name as well as its supply of water; the brook serving as the feeder to the canal . . . running northerly . . . proceeds to Gerrard's Bridge and St. Helen's where it terminates.' Priestley also gives some of the principal cargoes as being coal 'to the plate glass manufactory near Warrington'. The Sankey Brook Navigation was a pioneer canal, being a completely artificial waterway, not a river navigation. This engraving is dated 1879 and depicts the sheet and rolled plate glassworks, collieries and brickworks of Messrs Pilkington Brothers, as well as a number of rigged flats.

112 The Sankey Brook Navigation was later known as the St Helen's Canal, being taken over by the LNWR in 1864. Unlike many such takeovers, this one involved an undertaking on the railway company's part to improve the canal. The coal traffic gradually went over to the railways, but slowly chemical factories came to the area, and in 1900 the canal was still carrying over 300,000 tons of cargo a year. It was finally abandoned in 1963, having

closed in 1959. Some of the last cargo be carried went to the Sankey Sugar Company at Earlestown by Sankey Viaduct. Prior to that some cargoes of malt seen here were brought up to Sankey Bridges, this picture having been taken there in December 1956. While most of the major bridges on the navigation were swing bridges, this on carrying the Liverpool to Warrington road is a lift bridge. This motor craft, the *Ellesweir* was at this time owned b Burtons of Liverpool, but had been built in 1924 at Yarwoods of Northwi as a steam barge. The coming of the chemical works caused their own problems. Edwin Pratt wrote in 1906: 'Early in the seventies the canal becam practically a wreck, owing to the mort on the walls having been destroyed by the chemicals in the water which the manufactories had drained into the canal. In addition, there was an overflow into the Sankey Brook, and i times of flood the water flowed over t meadows, and thousands of acres wer rendered barren. The London and North-Western Railway Company, who owned the Canal, went to great expense in litigation, and obtained an injunction against the manufacturers, and in the result they had to purchase all the meadows outright, as the quickest way of settling the question o compensation. The Company rebuilt all the walls and some of the locks. . . .

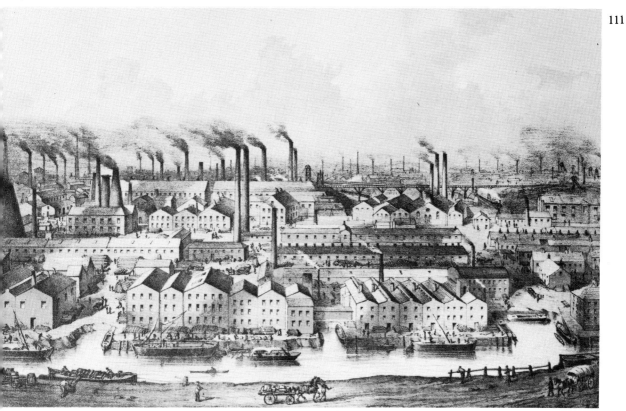

113

SANTA ROSA

114

CANAL VIEW SANRE

13/114 These two pictures were taken in 1906 at the time of the launch of the United Alkali Company's jigger at *Santa Rosa*. She was built at Clare and Ridgway's yard at Sankey Bridges on the St Helen's Canal. Clare and Ridgeway were well known as builders of flats in that area. The *Santa Rosa* was built for the North Wales limestone trade to United Alkali's Fleetwood soda plant, usually returning to Liverpool with soda products for export. She would not have traded over the St Helen's Canal on which she was built. This then is another example of a shipyard on a canal, building sea-going vessels.

115 If the Sankey Brook cannot claim to be the first canal, then it must have been the first artificial waterway to use a steam-powered boat. Priestley in 1831 says 'an experiment of propelling vessels by steam was tried upon this canal as early as 1797, when a loaded barge was worked up and down by a steam engine on board for a distance of 20 miles; but, singular as it may appear, to this time vessels have continued to be towed upon it by manual labour.' Steam power of a different sort was applied many years later for this dredger. It was built by Priestman of Hull as a grab dredger, and was delivered to the LNWR in 1881 for the St Helen's Canal. The steam plant on the crane also propelled the hull by a shaft through the centre of the slewing ring with a bevel drive to the propeller. Dredger *Widnes* is seen here on 5 April 1959 in Winwick dry dock attached to the canal company's yard; the boat was in the process of being broken up.

6   For many centuries people had
en trying to trade on the Rivers
ersey and Irwell to gain access to
anchester. An Act of Parliament was
ssed in 1721 to make these rivers
vigable, but it is not thought the
ute was opened satisfactorily until
36. It is interesting to note that the
oprietors were aware of the coal on
e estates of the Duke of Bridgewater,
in 1736 an Act of Parliament was
ssed allowing them to make the
orsley Brook navigable for two miles
om the River Irwell up towards the
uke's mines at Worsley. This
aterway was never built although, of
urse, at one time it did have the
uke's approval. Instead, as we all
ow, his son, the second Duke, built
s own canal to Manchester. This
otograph of Mode Wheel lock on the
ersey and Irwell navigation, was
ken in 1888 just a year or so before it
as demolished to make way for the
anchester Ship Canal. It is clear from
e state of the water that pollution was
problem even at that time.

117   One of the features of the Duke of
Bridgewater's canal was the aqueduct at
Barton, which carried the new
waterway at a height of 39ft over the
Mersey and Irwell Navigation. When
the plans for this aqueduct were first
put forward, one eminent engineer
apocryphally remarked that he had
'often heard of castles in the air; but
never before had he seen where any of
them were to be erected.' When opened
it was hailed as a wonder of the world.
Because of the building of the
Manchester Ship Canal in the 1890s,
Brindley's aqueduct had to be
demolished and it was replaced by the
possibly equally remarkable Barton
Swing Aqueduct. Very few pictures of
the original structure seem to have
survived, but this one shows it in the
distance. It was taken by a Manchester
Ship Canal photographer recording the
progress of that canal's construction.
Here, then, is the Mersey and Irwell
Navigation with a Manchester Ship
Canal contractor's railway running
along the far bank in preparation for
greater works to come.

118   When the Manchester Ship
Canal was opened in 1894 it had
eliminated most of the sections of the
Mersey and Irwell Navigation, then
known as the Runcorn and Latchford
Canal. The remaining lengths were
then used purely as a cut from the
Mersey to the Ship Canal. The Mersey
Flat seen here is the *Raven* owned by
the United Alkali Company; it was
built at Northwich in 1858, and is
pictured on the truncated length of the
Runcorn and Latchford.

119 The section of the Runcorn and
Latchford Canal that remained was
often called the Black Bear Canal. It
carried traffic until recently, although it
has now been filled in. The craft seen
here tied up on the Black Bear Canal
belong to the Bridgewater Department
of the Manchester Ship Canal, they
were built in the early 1950s at
Northwich on the River Weaver. The
motor craft (centre) could carry 80 tons,
and all had names beginning with *par*.
The dumb barges could carry 114 tons,
and all had the suffix *mere*.

120   The 45½-mile Chesterfield Canal
was finally opened in 1777 connecting
the town of that name with the River
Trent at Stockwith Junction. It was a
heavily locked line, having sixty-five
locks in all, plus two tunnels. The
proprietors decided to meet the railway
mania by involving themselves heavily
in the formation of the Manchester and
Lincoln Union Railway Company. In
1848 the railway company did much
work to improve the canal having
found . . .'in consequence of the
ordinary repairs having been for many
years grossly neglected, and the canal
becoming almost impassable in many
places but it is satisfactory to find that
this outlay is already being returned by
means of the increasing trade.' This
photograph taken around 1900 shows
part of a three-lock riser in the
Norwood Flight some eleven or so
miles down from Chesterfield. The
buildings on the right are a water-
power sawmill.

121 For its first half mile, the Chesterfield Canal ran down the River Rother, which also acted as a feeder for the upper stretches. This photograph shows the head of navigation and Chesterfield Basin as it was prior to 1890. The River Rother is in the foreground. The basin is protected by a flood lock which would be closed should the river level rise unduly. As can be seen, Chesterfield Basin was very attractive, with warehouses on the left, and a covered loading area under the warehouse at the end. The wharfside crane can also be seen.

122 The first lock down the Chesterfield Canal was Ford Lane, or Tapton Lock, and this photograph of 1890 shows this lock and cottage. It is a pity we cannot read the two notices affixed to the cottage wall under the eaves, as they obviously refer to the canal — would one have been a toll board? The top section of the canal is still used as a watercourse taking water from the River Rother to Staveley Iron Works. The top lock gate here is still in situ and is used as a weir on the commercial water channel.

123 During its life the canal passed into the hands of the Great Central Railway, and later the London and North Eastern Railway. Dredging is an important part of any canal maintenance programme. Here we see how a 70ft horse-drawn narrow boat has been converted into a steam powered dredger. Unusually, the boat is not equipped with side pontoons as these would make it much more stable when at work. The dredger is unloading into crude mud hoppers which would have been towed away for emptying elsewhere. Unless there was a regular chain of empty boats awaiting filling, dredging could prove to be a slow and expensive process. This is a problem which troubles British Waterways to this day.

124 The Louth Navigation was completed in 1770, using part of the bed of the River Lud. It connected the Lincolnshire town of Louth with the River Humber, 11½ miles away. The principal traffic was coal and timber to the estuary. The craft using it were nearly all river-going Humber keels. Due to the shallow approaches from river to canal (a 3½ mile channel, marked by beacons), fully loaded keels drawing 5ft 6in could only enter during one week on a spring tide. This must have seriously hampered the prosperity of the waterway. Traffic ceased during World War I. Here we see an unladen Humber keel at Tetney Lock in 1908. The clinker build of the hull is very apparent in this photograph. The accompanying coggie or cog-boat is secured to the stern and the lee-boards are clearly shown. These lee-boards grip the water when working to windward, in the same way as a centre board of a sailing dinghy. Often when trading onto narrow inland waterways the coggie boat, lee-boards, masts and sails were left at the entrance to the navigation as they would have been more of a hindrance than a help.

125 The small cinque port of Rye on the Sussex coast must have been typical of many of Britain's small tidal harbours. Two rivers ran down to the sea at Rye, the Rother and the Brede. The Rother had been used for trade from very early times; the stone for building Bodiam Castle, for example, said to have come in this way. The boats trading above Rye were a version of the river barge and only found in the area. They had to be under 45ft long by 12ft beam to pass through the tidal sluice lock known as Scots Float Sluice. They were locally made, built of wood and the smaller ones drew 3ft when loaded with 20 tons of cargo. They had pointed sterns and were lug-sail rigged. This photograph of two of them was taken around 1910 on the tidal reaches of the river. It is thought that none of them survived into the 1950s.

126

127

26 Trade continued on the Rother up to Newenden, some 12¼ miles inland, until 1909. This photograph was taken just prior to that date, and shows the head of the navigation at Newenden Bridge. The principal cargoes carried were coal, timber, some agricultural products and manure, also shingle from the foreshore for road resurfacing. Much of the incoming timber was for the sawmill on the left of the picture. Here you see a portable steam engine which would have been used for driving the saw benches. Note also the barge under sail, or at least with the sail hoisted. The Royal Military Canal built in 1806 joined the Rother above Rye and although it was built primarily for defence purposes, barges did move on it carrying essential military supplies, the last trade on it being in 1909.

127 The River Brede was navigable for 8 miles inland from Rye, the river running back almost parallel to the coast towards Hastings. One of the principal cargoes was coal, carried up to Brede Bridge for use in the Hastings and St Leonards Waterworks. On two consecutive days each fortnight water conditions were right for 20-ton barges to come up to the waterworks wharf, the boats normally being quanted or bow-hauled. This is a very good view of the stern of a Rye river barge, *Victoria* of Rye, being unloaded by the wharf steam crane. It is quite obvious from this picture that this is the limit of navigation on the river.

128 Coal was loaded into 4 ton wagons running on an 18in gauge steam-hauled tramway. On arrival at the waterworks a hydraulic hoist tipped the coal into a 500-ton capacity coal store. Here we see the locomotive (an 0-4-0 saddle tank), trucks and crew of this tramway. By 1928 it was impossible to bring barges up the river, due to deterioration in the navigation, so coal had to come by rail to Coleham Holt. Thence it was transferred by horse and cart to the tramway. Later a hard road was built from the main line to the waterworks down the route of part of the tramway, which was then abandoned.

129 The River Wye was at one time navigable for 99 miles inland from its junction with the River Severn below Chepstow to Hay on Wye, although the following extract from Priestley shows it could be fraught with danger: '. . . the navigation, however, of the lower part of this river is, during spring tides and when the wind blows fresh from the south west, attended with no inconsiderable risk, as the tide, at its confluence with the Severn, sometimes reaches the extraordinary perpendicular elevation of 60 feet, [can this be correct?] which necessarily causes a tremendous and overpowering rush of water up the narrow channel of the Wye.' He also failed to report on the dependence on flood water for traffic up to Hereford and beyond. The rapids at Monnington did not help, the boats having to be hauled up these with the aid of a block and tackle. Even low down the river a Wye barge which only took 10 tons of cargo needed a team of thirty-two men to move it, eight at a time, on one recorded voyage in 1847. The engraving shows the bridge carrying the Newport, Abergavenny and Hereford Railway over the river at Hereford, possibly soon after the railway opened in 1854. Although a steam tug was known to be operating on the river in the late 1820s she was soon sold. Nothing is known of the steam paddle boat in this picture, which looks like a private launch as she is too small to carry much cargo. The river below Hereford became unnavigable soon after this and by 1904 *Bradshaw* was only quoting it from Bigsweir Bridge, some four miles above Tintern.

130 While Priestley claimed there was no bore, *Bradshaw* in 1904 said 'there is, as a rule, no "bore" or tidal wave formed in the river by the first of the flood tides but in summer, when there is very little land water coming down, a high spring tide will sometimes cause one to rise above Chepstow.' Because navigation was so uncertain the railways very quickly took away the majority of the trade and *Bradshaw* again reveals in 1904: 'the river is navigable to Chepstow on all tides. The course of the river above Chepstow is very tortuous and the numerous fishing weirs placed partially across the river cause rapids, which are very dangerous to navigation, unless conducted on the top of the tide. There is a small general trade done up to Chepstow: stone is brought down from Lancaut quarries, and timber from Brock Weir. The opening of the Wye Valley Railway in 1876 caused the bulk of the trade on the river to cease.' This is the wharf at Chepstow in around 1900.

130

Chepstow Castle

a distributing port for cargoes going inland. Traffic for the upper reaches of the Severn was usually taken to Bewdley for transhipment to shallower drafted vessels for onward transmission. The coming of the canals altered the pattern of trading on the river, and with the completion of the Staffordshire and Worcestershire Canal which joined the river at Stourport, a canal-made town, the importance of trade on the upper reaches declined. This photograph, thought to have been taken around 1880 at Bewdley, shows just part of the wharf area. The boat is one of the Severn narrow-boats known in that area as long boats. They were the largest narrow-boats built, carrying up to 45 tons of cargo on a draft of 3ft 9in. Although mainly used on the Severn, they did trade inland up the connecting canals to the Birmingham Canal Navigation. Many of these were not family boats as the Severn boatmen often lived ashore. They lived at Gloucester and were expert rivermen — a clan of boatmen on their own. Downstream is a demasted Severn trow, most probably then being used as a dumb barge.

131 At one time the River Severn was a principal inland artery of the country, and was navigable 178 miles inland to Pool Quay below Welshpool in Montgomeryshire, and over this length it fell 225ft. The port of Bristol acted as

FLOOD at BEWDLEY
23 Jan: 1899

2 The problem with any river navigation is its susceptibility to flood drought. Floods on the River Severn are some of the most devastating in the country, as this picture of Bewdley in 1899 clearly shows. For reasons quite unknown, the photographer has captioned this picture twice showing the floods to be 23 January 1899 and/or February 1899. In the previous picture it was noticeable how the houses had been built up to avoid flooding, but here it has been proved that they are not high enough, even though there is a massive river wall between them and the river, as well as the width of a good road. The landing stages are clearly an adaptation of a narrowboat, while the swimming pool opposite is built around two narrowboats, both still equipped with rudders; one looks still to have its tiller as well. The narrowboat tied up to the landing stages has its towing mast erect, complete with sheave pulley block and many yards of line around the fore-end and the cabin top. The reason for this was that towing from the bank of a river required much more line than a similar operation on a narrow canal.

133 While coal had been a major cargo down the river from parts of Shropshire, the growth of the iron industry at Coalbrookdale meant that trade increased a great deal, and this part of the river became a focal point. Because industrial activity was so intense on both sides of the gorge, a bridge was constructed and opened in 1781, the Iron Bridge. The bridge was designed to allow masted river traffic to pass underneath. This view, looking downstream, was taken in 1892, and the heavily laden trow is not moored at one of the recognised wharves of the area. This is one of the smaller up-river trows and would not normally have traded below Gloucester. In recent years £250,000 has had to be spent in rebuilding the abutments on either side of the Iron Bridge due to the gradual slipping of the valley sides. The same movement has taken place in other parts of the gorge with the result that the bed of the river has gradually risen. This is one of the reasons why navigation became so difficult in the 1800s due to the forming of rapids.

134 At Dale End, Coalbrookdale, stands this splendid Gothic-style warehouse. This was Loadcroft wharf, one of the principal wharves on the river at that time. The exact date of this photograph is not known, but it is thought to be as early as the 1860s. A fully rigged but unladen Severn trow lies at the wharf while a smaller unrigged version lies alongside. Again this is an up-river trow. Sometimes called 'frigates' they carried up to 80 tons, but there were also many smaller ones carrying 30 tons on a 3ft loaded draught. Goods for loading come out of the warehouse on a small mixed-gauge tramway, the rails and trucks of which can be clearly seen. The central pillared crane with strutted jib is typical of wharf cranes. Most of the products of the Darby foundries in Coalbrookdale would have been shipped out from this wharf. Besides the trows there was another type of craft not often written up — a large raft called a flote or drag, which had in the past been used for really heavy or bulky cargoes. These would have been floated downstream when the river was in flood. It is known that some of the huge castings required for beam engine cylinders, made at Abraham Darby's works in Coalbrookdale, went down-river on such rafts.

135 The Severn trow was a boat built for use over the whole of the Severn Navigation and it also traded down the coast on either side of the Bristol Channel. The trows had a flat bottom with a rounded bilge and external keel because of frequent grounding, and had a main and top mast and sometimes a mizzen as well. They were built at many different yards, but one of those furthest inland was opposite the Loadcroft wharf at Dale End, Coalbrookdale. Known as the Bower Yard, it continued building until the 1850s. Again the date of this photograph is uncertain, but it could be that this was one of the last of these trows to have been built here, or perhaps it had just had a re-fit. In 1787 iron master John Wilkinson launched a barge of 30-ton capacity, made of iron at Willey Wharf. This is thought to have been successful. Little has been written about it, but presumably it was used as a dumbbarge and not equipped for sailing. The majority of Severn trows were built of wood, though Benjamin Banks of Stourport had a fleet of ten iron trows.

136 The last barge to trade to Shrewsbury came in 1862 and by this time there was no trade to Pool Quay. Unfortunately, the date of this engraving of Shrewsbury bridge is not known. The problem with the Severn was that it never had any controlling commissioners, so very little work was ever done to aid navigation. In times of severe flood, navigation was impossible, and in times of drought boats were stuck for days on the shallows. A boat going downstream would either sail or use the current, but upstream it would have to be bow hauled by teams of men. Horses could not be used until a series of Acts of Parliament were passed between 1772 and 1811 which allowed a towing path suitable for horses to be constructed, between Shrewsbury and Gloucester. Previous to this the bow haulier reigned supreme on the upper river, some 150 being employed around 1800. The Mug House Inn at Bewdley was a favourite place for barge owners going upstream to pick up their gang of hauliers. It is said the terms for the haulage were usually sealed with a mug of beer.

137 Ferries have always been a feature of any river navigation where passengers and light cargoes can be carried across at a point where there is no bridge. This is the Coalport ferry, a mile or so below the great Iron Bridge. The ferry boat is possibly a converted trow onto which a very crude rear cabin has been built for shelter in really inclement weather. The boat is propelled by the river current, using a guiding rope from the mast to the bank; a large rudder helps with steerage. There used to be several of these ferries on the Severn, and recently one has been revived by the Severn Valley Railway, at Hampton Loade. The picture is thought to date from around 1880 and on the right side of the photograph can be seen the Hay inclined plane, which carried tub boats down from the Shropshire Canal to the banks of the River Severn. This incline finally closed in 1894. Because transhipment to river vessels was difficult at this point, a short canal was built from the bottom of the plane, parallel to the river to Coalport — hence the name, and the principal cargoes carried for many years were coal and pig iron. It was also intended to develop the river bank as a 'new town', with canal access to the factories

135

INDEX TO PART 1